GW01007432

12.9.89

hope you
enjoy this book
love your hen
xx

open top STYLE

open top STYLE

GRAHAM ROBSON

A QUINTET BOOK

Published by New Burlington Books
6 Blundell Street
London N7 9BH

ISBN 1-85348-036-3

This book was designed and produced by
Quintet Publishing Limited
6 Blundell Street
London N7 9BH

Art Director: Peter Bridgewater
Designer: Jean Foley
Editors: Paul Berman, Shaun Barrington

Typeset in Great Britain by
Central Southern Typesetters, Eastbourne
Manufactured in Hong Kong by Regent
Publishing Services Limited
Printed in Hong Kong by Leefung-Asco
Printers Limited

CONTENTS

INTRODUCTION

The attraction of open-top motoring is ideally summed up by an advert run by BL for the Triumph TR7 Convertible. A side view of the car, with soft-top furled, simply showed an arrow pointing upwards, with the punchline: 'Headroom: 93 million miles'. Quite simply, in an open-top car there is, or should be, no barrier between the driver and the rest of the world.

This book, in fact, is a celebration of a type of car which looked set to disappear ten years ago – the open-top type. Since then, of course, there has been a real revival, and a great deal of variety is once again on offer.

In the beginning, cars were sometimes known as 'horseless-carriages', and *all* of them were open-top types of one sort or another. Quite clearly, their styles had evolved from the coachwork of horse-drawn carriages of an earlier era.

In later years, as tastes changed, and the coachbuilder's art was refined to take account of this, more and more closed cars were sold, but an increasing variety of convertible machines also became available.

Because one man's convertible is another man's drophead coupe, one country's roadster is another country's tourer, there are two spellings of Spider/Spyder, and many other derivations on the De Ville, Landaulette, Cabriolet and Targa-roof theme, I am not about to offer a rigid definition of the convertible car. Accordingly, I have covered several different types of car in which the roof can be folded, removed, hinged – or has never actually been fitted. For that reason, therefore, a Rolls-Royce Landaulette is as much of an open-top as a Fiat X1/9, and a Cadillac Allanté is just as interesting as a Morris Minor 1000.

Ten years ago, the pundits were ready to write off the open-top car, blaming such diverse influences as United States safety legislation and the increased performance of the cars themselves, but it was never as simple as that.

Roll-over safety and the maintenance of a girl's hairstyle were both significant, of course, but not vital. The main reasons for the decline were connected with the arrival of unit-construction body/chassis units, and with the increased cost of producing limited-production specialist coachwork. Originally it was quite straightforward to produce a special body, usually based on a wood-frame skeleton, if a separate chassis provided almost all the structural stiffness. However, it was much more complicated, and costly, if there was *no* separate chassis, so that a unit-construction saloon car shell had to be re-engineered to provide open-top motoring.

Unit-construction shells were introduced for mass-production cars in the 1930s, and became dominant within 20 years. By the 1960s, open-top motoring was rapidly becoming confined to sports cars, and to the *very* expensive type of coachbuilt machine. Then, as the 1970s progressed, it began to seem that open-top cars would soon be outlawed in the USA, which meant that newly introduced sports cars like the Triumph TR7 and the Jaguar XJ-S

RIGHT In the late 1930s, the BMW 328 sports car was one of the most desirable open-top cars in the world. Among its advanced features were a powerful 6-cylinder engine, and independent front suspension. The post-war Bristol was inspired by this German car.

were closed coupes, and that nothing new was coming along to replace well-loved 'classics' like the Alfa Romeo Giulia Spider and the MG MGB.

When General Motors built the last of its convertibles (Cadillac Eldorados) in 1976, pessimists were ready to write off the open-top car for good. Open-top monocoques like the MG MGB, and the Mercedes-Benz 450SL, it was suggested, were now dinosaurs, the last of the line, and the best that could be expected in the 1980s was a Porsche-style 'Targa' top, or a 'removable-roof' model like the Ferrari 308GTS.

And so it seemed – until the West Germans immediately started a new trend, with the launch of the smart new 3-Series BMW (1977) and Golf (1979) Cabriolets, both of which were based on unit-construction shells. Two years later BL launched the Triumph TR7 Convertible, a conversion of the Coupe, and the bandwagon began to roll.

The public's reaction was enthusiastic, and this was enough to encourage other makers to follow suit. Before long, other open-top cars, like the Peugeot 205 CTi, and the Porsche 911 Cabriolet, were launched, Jaguar produced an XJ-S Cabriolet, while North American makers such as Cadillac and Chrysler turned to Italy for expertise in producing large open-top models.

By the late 1980s, motoring included open-top cars as tiny as the Yugo 55 Cabriolet and as large and glossy as the Rolls-Royce Corniche, as middle-of-the road as the Ford Escort XR3i Cabriolet, and as excitingly high-performance as the Porsche 911 Turbo Cabriolet. Open-top motoring was fashionable once again, and as long as the air is still fit to breathe, its future should be assured.

GRAHAM ROBSON

RIGHT A famous Jaguar makes off, once again, for the open road. Ian Appleyard's twin-cam six-cylinder XK120 was *the* most successful rally car of the early 1950s.

ABOVE, FAR RIGHT Behind the wheel of a 1928 Bugatti Type 43; the world's first 100mph production car is an excellent example of one very obvious attraction of early open-top motoring – its association with racing. The Type 43 used a very slightly detuned version of the Type 35B Grand Prix car's supercharged 2.3-litre straight-eight engine. It is also notorious as the car that caused the death of the dancer Isadora Duncan, whose long scarf became entangled in the wire wheels as she sped along.

BELOW, FAR RIGHT Every car styled by Sir William Lyons between the 1920s and the 1970s had sinuous lines. This was the famous late-1930s SS100, complete with twin spare wheels, a 'slab' tank, and removable side-curtains. Even when parked at the kerbside it looked as if it was doing 60mph.

ALFA ROMEO GIULIA SPIDER

PRODUCTION SPAN
1966 to date

ENGINE
4-cyl, 2 ohc

CAPACITY
79-120 CID/1290cc–1964cc

MAXIMUM POWER
89bhp to 122bhp, depending on engine

CHASSIS/SUSPENSION
Steel platform/ monocoque, coil spring/ wishbone ifs, live axle and coil spring rear

BODY STYLE
2 seater DHC, by Pininfarina

TOP SPEED
105mph/169kph to 120mph/193kph, depending on engine

0-60MPH
10.5 seconds to 8.8 seconds, depending on engine

There is a long history of sumptuously styled open-top cars at Alfa Romeo. In the early days of this Italian company, the cars had separate-chassis construction and it was easy to provide special coachwork, but even when more complex monocoque (unit-body) construction was adopted after the Second World War, the tradition was maintained.

In the 1950s, Alfa Romeo launched a series of smaller engined cars, and expanded considerably. The first of all these cars was the Giulietta, which had an advanced 1.3-litre/79 CID four-cylinder engine, with twin overhead camshaft valve gear. Bertone styled a coupe version of this car, while Pininfarina styled the open-top Spider.

Alfa Romeo introduced the first of the four-door unit-body Giulia saloons in 1962, using a 1.6-litre/96 CID version of the Giulietta's engine. Although it was inevitable that coupe and Spider versions would be launched, the first open-top Giulia, called the 1600 Spider, did not appear until 1966.

As before, Pininfarina had styled, and would build, the two-seater bodies for the Spider (the shape was actually the last credited to Battista Pininfarina himself), on a shortened version of the Giulia's floorpan, but with all the same chassis and running gear. All the sporty Giulias had a five-speed transmission.

In its original form, the new car had a contoured 'scallop' running along its flanks, and a long tapering tail, with the traditional Alfa radiator style up front. It was available with an optional, removable, hardtop, and was originally called 'Duetto' as the result of a public competition to find a suitable name. Like all good Italian sports cars should, the Duetto had an urgent character, a free-revving engine, and a great deal of *brio* – it was the sort of car one always used with the top down, even if it was raining!

From 1969 the Spider was re-styled, with a sharply cut-off and shortened tail style, plus a more modern facia and many other styling re-touches. At the same time the engine was enlarged to 1.8-litre/108 CID. This was the start of a period of rapid permutation at Alfa Romeo, for in the next few years 1.3-litre/79 CID *and* 2.0-litre/120 CID versions of the same engine were all made available in this body shell.

Naturally this car sold well in the United States where, by the mid-1970s, it needed a fuel-injected version of the 2.0-litre/120 CID engine to keep apace with the latest exhaust emission laws. By the late 1970s, the Spider had been withdrawn from all but that market, where it continued to sell, and be enjoyed, into the 1980s.

Just when it seemed that the Spider was coasting on towards an honourable retirement, in 1986 Pininfarina treated it to a substantial facelift, complete with new front and rear spoilers, and skirts along the flanks. This, to say the least, was a controversial move, which seemed to destroy the original elegance without making the facelift worthwhile.

TOP The Alfa Spider's instrument panel, like the rest of the car's design, was functional without being flash. This was a 1982 model, with the 2.0-litre engine. Did the driver really *need* to know any more than this?

ABOVE Alfa Romeo's famous four-cylinder twin-cam engine was first seen as a 1.3-litre unit in the 1950s. By the early 1980s, it produced more than 120bhp in 2.0-litre form.

ABOVE RIGHT The early Spiders were called 'Duetto', and had a long and rounded tail, but from 1969 Pininfarina modified the design, by cutting the tail short. This was a 1978 model. The long sloping nose and the distinctively sculptured sides of this design remained the same, however, for more than 20 years.

BELOW RIGHT Some designs are so 'classic' that they do not need to be re-designed as the years pass by. Twelve years after it was launched the Alfa Romeo Giulia Spider was just as elegant, and up-to-the-minute, as always.

15225-EE

ASTON MARTIN VOLANTE

PRODUCTION SPAN
1978 to date

ENGINE
V8, 2 ohc

CAPACITY
326 CID/5340cc

MAXIMUM POWER
309bhp (Vantage 406bhp)

CHASSIS/SUSPENSION
Steel platform, coil spring/ wishbone ifs, De Dion and coil spring rear

BODY STYLE
2+2 DHC, by Aston Martin

TOP SPEED
145mph/233kph (Vantage 170mph/273kph)

0-60MPH
6.2 seconds (Vantage 5.4 seconds)

The original Aston Martin DBS appeared in 1967, as a fastback coupe with a six-cylinder engine, but the enormously powerful 5.3-litre/326 CID V8 engine for which it had been designed made its appearance two years later. That engine, and the same basic body style, whether in closed or open-top form, were to form the basis of every Aston Martin produced in the next two decades. There was one name change, from DBS-V8, to mere 'V8', in 1972, and minor styling changes from time to time.

Even in standard-engined form it could beat 140mph/ 225kph, and if the fearsomely fast 'Vantage' version was ordered that top speed rose to around 170mph/273kph. In spite of its weight and bulk, it handled extremely well, though the fuel consumption was heavy. There was a choice between five-speed manual, or three-speed automatic transmissions, and the V8 was one of the few production cars in the world to use De Dion rear suspension.

Aston Martin, like other specialist car makers, always liked to have a convertible derivative of all its cars, and had first launched a 'Volante' version (which was Aston Martin's own special name for a soft-top car) of the previous range in the 1960s. It was not until 1978, however – 11 years after the coupe had first appeared – that the company offered the V8-engined Volante model.

The V8-engined car was based on a solidly engineered steel platform chassis which, because it was effectively hand-built, featured many small pressings or fabrications. Much of the body shell was steel, but many skin panels were in aluminium alloy, the whole being an intriguing blend of machine-made pressings, hand-dressed, matched, and welded together at the Aston Martin factory at Newport Pagnell. Because it was a large and wide car, the coupe was a full four-seater.

The V8 Volante, launched in June 1978, had the same basic style as the coupe, but naturally featured a power-operated soft-top, and had its floorpan stiffened to restore the rigidity of the 'chassis'. Volantes, it seemed, would take up to three months to build, and the first USA price was set at no less than $66,000. Although four full-sized seats (leather-trimmed, of course) were still provided, the folding top had encroached on the boot space, which was reduced from 8.6 cu. ft. to a mere 5.1 cu. ft.

The soft-top was, as you might expect, beautifully tailored, and when erect it turned the Volante into a snug, if somewhat claustrophobic, two-door saloon. It was just as carefully built as a Rolls-Royce. In any case a customer had a right to expect this, as he was paying similar prices.

At first the Volante was only available with the standard engine, but from 1986 an extra version, complete with deep front spoiler, was offered with the Vantage engine.

Aston Martin, which had been owned by a succession of hopeful entrepreneurs in the 1970s and 1980s, was finally taken over by the Ford Motor Co. Ltd. in 1987.

ABOVE The classic modern Aston Martin shape started life as a closed coupe in 1967; the convertible Volante followed in 1978.

ABOVE Soft top up, or soft top down, this is a brutally impressive style. The later Volantes were also offered with the most powerful Vantage engine, and with these styling changes.

LEFT What could be better – wood, British leather, a padded steering wheel, and a speedometer reading to unimaginable levels.

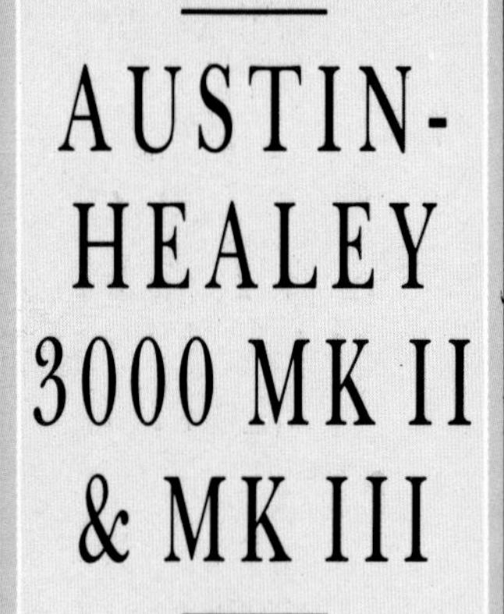

AUSTIN-HEALEY 3000 MK II & MK III

PRODUCTION SPAN
1962–1967

ENGINE
6-cyl, ohv

CAPACITY
178 CID/2912cc

MAXIMUM POWER
131bhp/148bhp

CHASSIS/SUSPENSION
Ladder-style frame, steel body shell welded on assembly, coil spring/ wishbone ifs, live axle and half-elliptic leaf spring rear

BODY STYLE
2+2 seater DHC, by Jensen/BMC

TOP SPEED
117mph/188kph; 121mph/195kph

0-60MPH
10.4 seconds/9.8 seconds

The Austin-Healey marque was born in 1952, and disappeared in 1970. In that time, only two different types of sports car – the small four-cylinder engined Sprite, and the larger 100/3000 range – were produced. Both were successful, and have a secure 'classic' reputation.

Donald Healey was already a famous motoring personality before he began building cars of his own design in 1946. The original 'Healeys' had Riley engines, but from 1952 the next generation was planned to use Austin engines. In a historic tie-up, his prototype Healey 100 was absorbed by the BMC combine, and the Austin-Healey marque was born.

At first the 'Big Healey' (as it eventually became known), had a four-cylinder engine, but BMC's new straight 'six' took over for 1957. This car, the 100 Six, became '3000' in 1959 with an enlarged engine, but it was not until 1962 that the body style was revised, and the true drop-head coupe was announced. All were simply built, reliable and fast.

All such Austin-Healeys were based on the same rugged chassis frame, to which the steel body shells were welded at the original assembly stage. From 1952 to 1962, however, these cars had detachable side curtains and a detachable soft-top. Some had two seats, and some were rather cramped 'occasional' 2+2 seaters. The four-cylinder cars had folding windscreens while the 'sixes' had fixed screens. All had the same graceful lines, a rather restricted ground clearance and a great deal of extrovert character. Somehow these were real he-men's cars, and have since been dubbed the last of the hairy-chested sports cars.

In 1962, the cabin was substantially re-engineered. There was a larger and curved windscreen, wind-up windows in the doors, a proper fold-away soft top with rigid rails above the door glasses and a zip-out rear window. Although all cars retained their small '+2' bucket rear seats, these had very restricted leg space, and were more useful for carrying luggage instead of people. A full-length tonneau cover was an optional extra, as was a detachable hardtop, though very few of the latter were actually sold.

Between 1962 and 1964 the rugged six-cylinder 2.9-litre/ 178 CID engine produced 131bhp, and the car retained the original oval-shaped instrument panel. From the beginning of 1964, until the last of the Big Healeys was built in the winter of 1967/1968, the model became Mk III.

Mk IIIs had a smart new facia style, with a wooden dashboard, a centre console between the seats and a fold-down luggage tray above the occasional rear seats. The engines were boosted to produce 148bhp, and the rear suspension was revised to give more accurate location of the axle.

During the 1960s the Austin-Healey was also developed, by the BMC factory, into a first-class competition car, supreme in high-speed rallies, and a very respectable performer in international motor racing. Many of these cars had light-alloy body panels, though all the road cars were built in pressed steel.

ABOVE The 'Big Healey' Mk III not only had wind-up windows, and a fold-down soft-top, but a wooden facia too.

RIGHT Even in the mid-1960s, the Healey 3000 retained the same basic lines as the original Austin-Healey 100 of 1952. The wind-up windows and the proper foldaway soft-top were added to the specification in 1962. This is a final-specification Mk III model.

INSERT, RIGHT From the front, the only way to differentiate a final-model 3000 Mk III from the original is by the separate side and turn indicator lamps.

LUU 655D
LUU 655D

BENTLEY CONTINENTAL, S-TYPE

PRODUCTION SPAN
1955–1965

ENGINE
6-cyl, ohv/V8, ohv

CAPACITY
298 CID/4887cc;
380 CID/6230cc

MAXIMUM POWER
Not quoted

CHASSIS/SUSPENSION
Ladder-style frame, cruciform braced, coil spring/wishbone ifs, live axle and half elliptic leaf spring rear

BODY STYLE
5 seater DHC, by various coachbuilders

TOP SPEED
(6-cyl) 119mph/192kph;
(V8) 113mph/182kph

0-60MPH
12.9 seconds/12.1 seconds

The original Bentley company had been absorbed by Rolls-Royce in 1931, and the first 'Continental' model was actually a sporting version of the Rolls-Royce Phantom II of the early 1930s. It was not until the early 1950s that the 'Continental' title was applied to a Bentley.

Starting in 1945, Rolls-Royce evolved a rationalized range of chassis, in which the Bentley marque was merely a more sporting version of the Rolls-Royce of the day. Then, as later, the engines' power output was not revealed – persistent enquirers were merely answered with the suave comment that it was 'sufficient' . . . .

The post-war Bentley of 1946, the Mk IV, was the very first to have what was called a 'standard steel' saloon car body, and a Rolls-Royce equivalent, the Silver Dawn, followed a few years later.

There was still, it seemed, a healthy demand for high-performance Bentleys with a sporting character, and sleek bodywork produced by independent coachbuilders. On the R-Type chassis, therefore, the first of the Bentley Continentals was made available in 1952, and it set a trend followed in 1955 by the S-Type Continental, and during the 1970s by the Corniche.

Compared with a standard-steel Bentley, a Continental had special coachwork, still with four/five seater accommodation, and usually with two doors. Most of the cars were closed coupes, but an increasing number were ordered with convertible coachwork. Although many Bentley saloons were still chauffeur-driven, the Continental was essentially a driver's car.

Customers could direct the rolling chassis to the coachbuilder of their choice, but it was usually H. J. Mulliner, Park Ward, and James Young who got the business. Park Ward had been a Rolls-Royce subsidiary since the late 1930s, and H. J. Mulliner joined them in 1959.

Compared with the R-Type, the S-Type had a new chassis, a longer wheelbase, yet no more passenger accommodation. For the first four years the cars were powered by the long-established 4.9-litre/298 CID straight six-cylinder engine, but from late 1959 a new light-alloy V8 engine took over. Except for a very few 1955/1956 models, all had the Rolls-Royce/GM automatic transmission. Every car had drum brakes, boosted by the famous Rolls-Royce mechanical servo.

The S-Types were all large, heavy and impressive machines, with power-operated soft tops, wind-down windows in the doors, and the highest possible standards of trim, decoration and seating. Prices were very high, but so were the standards of trim. The cars were certainly more carefully built than any other of the world's luxury machines available at the time. Although an S-Type Continental was a fast car if the driver insisted (and fuel consumption, at around 15/17 Imperial mpg was very reasonable), it was more usual to see these cars used for smooth and dignified transport, around town as well as on the open road.

RIGHT The Bentley Continental S1 was built between 1956 and 1959 and was the last of the Continentals to use a six cylinder engine (in line with 8:1 compression ratio); a V8 was used for the S2 and S3 models.

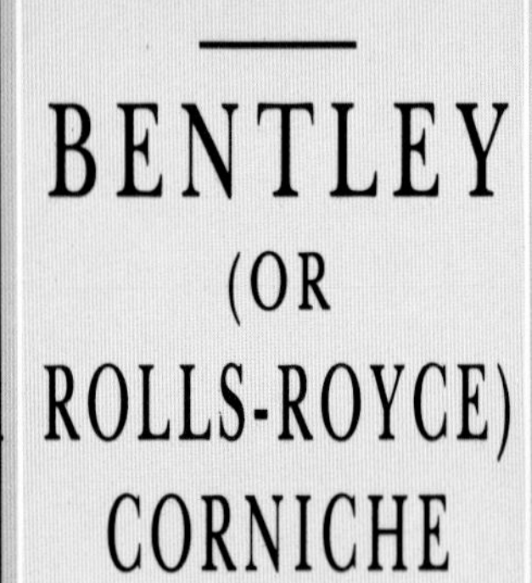

PRODUCTION SPAN
1971 to date

ENGINE
V8, ohv

CAPACITY
412 CID/6750cc

MAXIMUM POWER
Not quoted

CHASSIS/SUSPENSION
Pressed steel monocoque, coil spring/wishbone ifs, coil spring and semi trailing arm irs, with self-levelling

BODY STYLE
5 seater DHC, by Mulliner Park Ward

TOP SPEED
120mph/193kph;

0-60MPH
9.6 seconds

In 1965, the Rolls-Royce company introduced its first unit-body designs, the four-door, five-seater Silver Shadow, and near-identical Bentley T-Series models. Except for the use of the V8 engine, and a modified version of the existing automatic transmission, it was completely different from the old separate-chassis models. Among its notable chassis features were all-independent suspension incorporating self-levelling, four-wheel disc brakes; and power-assistance, it seemed, for just about everything.

The specialist coachbuilders greeted this new range with dismay, for it was going to be extremely costly to design different coachwork for such a model. Only James Young persevered, building a number of two-door saloons, but they then withdrew from the market. Henceforth it would only be practical for Rolls-Royce's own subsidiary, the merged Mulliner Park Ward company, to design and build a different style.

Starting in March 1966, MPW offered a smart two-door saloon version of these cars, and from the autumn of 1967 a convertible version of the same style. In each case, the Silver Shadow's underpan, structural members, and all the suspension, engine and running gear were retained, while the superstructure was new.

Although it was unmistakably based upon the Silver Shadow/T-Series, the new design was significantly lower, and had a dropped-waistline style which was not to be changed for at least 20 years. In 1971, with no more than minor changes to the design – including a 10 per cent more powerful engine and a different facia – the car was renamed Corniche, and was sold as a Bentley or a Rolls-Royce.

As you might expect from a modern Bentley/Rolls-Royce, the Corniche was technically advanced, and carefully hand-built. Although engine power was never revealed it was probably about 200/220bhp, this being quite 'sufficient' to push a 5,200lb/2,358kg car up to 120mph/193kph. There was four-seater accommodation, with great expanses of real leather and pile carpeting in evidence, the convertible soft top was not only lined, but padded, and the whole car took 20/24 *weeks* to be built; one whole week was needed to manufacture and 'tailor' the folding top itself.

Throughout the 1970s, every development change made to the saloons was also made to the Corniches. These changes included different and more compliant front suspension, re-designed rear suspension, power-assisted rack and pinion steering, and two-level air-conditioning, but the styling was never changed.

Even though the Silver Shadow/T-Series gave way to the new Silver Spirit/Mulsanne family in 1980, and the saloon version of the Corniche was dropped in 1981, the convertible stayed on into the late 1980s. From mid-1984, the Bentley-badged version was renamed Continental, thus reviving a famous name, but the Rolls-Royce persisted as a Corniche. UK prices, by 1987, had exceeded £100,000.

RIGHT Only Mulliner Park Ward could have made such an elegant drophead conversion job of the Rolls Royce Silver Shadow design. The Corniche was launched in 1971 and is still being built in the late 1980s.

BMW 3-SERIES CABRIOLET

PRODUCTION SPAN
1977 to date

ENGINE
4-cyl or 6-cyl, ohc

CAPACITY
96 CID/1574cc to
152 CID/2494cc

MAXIMUM POWER
90bhp to 170bhp,
depending on engine

CHASSIS/SUSPENSION
Pressed steel monocoque,
coil spring/MacPherson strut
ifs, coil spring and
semi-trailing arm irs

BODY STYLE
4 seater DHC, by Baur,
or by BMW since 1986

TOP SPEED
100mph/161kph to
130mph/209kph,
depending on engine

0-60MPH
13 seconds to 7.5 seconds,
depending on engine

The Second World War virtually wiped out BMW's business, and the company had to be painfully rebuilt in the 1940s and 1950s. A brand-new model with an overhead-camshaft engine, the 1500, came along in 1961, this being the start of a whole new family of modern BMW models.

In 1966 BMW introduced its first small/medium two-door saloon car, the unit-construction 1600-2. Like all such modern BMWs, this had independent suspension front *and* rear, and was immediately recognized by the characteristic kidney-shaped radiator grille. Even if BMW did not intend it to be so, it rapidly took on the mantle of a sports saloon, especially when the larger, 2-litre-engined versions were added to the range.

Eventually this car was sold with a whole variety of more powerful engines, and it was not supplanted by a new model, the first of the famous 3-Series cars, until 1975. A re-worked, but essentially similar 'Mark 2' 3-Series model came along in 1982, and sold even better than the original.

The first 3-Series range started with a four-cylinder 1.6-litre/96 CID engine, and worked its way up to a six-cylinder 2.3-litre/141 CID unit, with 143bhp, but the revised 3-Series also included a 170bhp 2.5-litre/152 CID 'six', not to mention diesel-engined alternatives.

In the 1970s, BMW was only equipped to build conventional saloon cars, so a demand for an open-top car had to be satisfied by co-operating with the Stuttgart-based company of Baur. It was not until 1977 that Baur unveiled its first 3-Series Cabriolets, and this car was to stay on the market until the mid-1980s.

Baur's Cabriolet was essentially a conversion of the 3-Series saloon, being virtually the same under the skin, below the waistline and ahead of the windscreen. Not only to give roll-over protection, but also to retain body shell rigidity, the Baur-designed Cabriolet had rigid cant-rails over the top of the doors, permanently fixed door pillars and a pressed 'roll-bar' over the passengers' heads. There was less space in the rear seats than in the equivalent saloons. Even so, this was a very popular, if high-priced, conversion, and one eventually offered for any of the differently powered 3-Series types.

BMW, however, was not completely satisfied with Baur's solution to the conversion; for some customers thought that it was rather too enclosed, and not enough of a 'fresh-air' machine. The company eventually designed its own car. The car's floorpan was significantly stiffened, and with the soft top furled there was complete all-round visibility. As on the Baur-built car, the soft top needed to be raised or lowered by hand. The factory-designed Cabriolet went on sale in 1986, and completely replaced the Baur unit.

ABOVE Every BMW, large or small, carries the same kidney-shaped grille, and the famous bonnet badge. The under-bumper spoiler was special to 325-engined types in 1986.

ABOVE BMW's 325i Cabriolet, which went on sale in 1986, was the first 'in house' design from BMW for many years. The previous soft-top 3-Series car was built by Baur, and had permanently fixed body sides and a permanent roll-bar over the seats.

LEFT The 3-Series Cabriolet might be an open-top car, but it has all the equipment of the Munich concern's saloons, including sumptuously trimmed seats.

Erecting the BMW's soft-top only took a few seconds. First it had to be lifted out of the locker behind the seats . . . . then the tail window surround had to be folded down . . . . and the result was a smooth and rounded profile.

OPPOSITE Not only was the BMW 3-Series Cabriolet a completely open-top car, but it was a full four-seater with a top speed of 120mph/193kph . . .

OPPOSITE, INSET . . . and this view of the six-cylinder fuel-injected overhead cam engine explains why.

CADILLAC CONVERTIBLES

PRODUCTION SPAN
1957–1964

ENGINE
V8, ohv

CAPACITY
365 CID/5.98 litres;
390 CID/6.38 litres;
429 CID/7.03 litres

MAXIMUM POWER
300/340bhp

CHASSIS/SUSPENSION
Separate steel chassis frame, coil spring and wishbone ifs, coil spring and radius arm beam rear

BODY STYLE
6 seater Convertible by Cadillac

TOP SPEED
(Typical) 115mph/185kph

0-60MPH
(Typical) 10.0 seconds approx

There have, of course, been many open-top Cadillacs, but none were quite so extraordinary, or so flamboyant, as those built in the 'age of the fins' period.

These cars were built at a time when the American nation as a whole, and General Motors in particular, was booming, self-confident and happy to indulge itself with extravagant consumer items. There was no functional need, and no economic reason, for giving fins to a Cadillac at this time but, what the heck, the stylists thought it made the cars look distinctive.

By the mid-1950s, Cadillac had thoroughly modernized its product line, and had an established range. All cars had V8 engines, usually with automatic transmission, and most models were in the 'Series 62' category, a group of cars which always included an open-top body option.

The Cadillac's running gear, too, had been rationalized. The cars had separate chassis frames, coil spring independent front suspension, and a live rear axle suspended on coil springs and located by radius arms. Mid-1950s engines were 365 CID/6.0-litre V8s, these being enlarged to 390 CID/6.4-litres for 1959, and to 429 CID/7.0-litres for 1964.

In the mid-1950s, Cadillac's convertible styles were all produced under the direction of Harley Earl, and it was not until the 1961 models appeared that his successor, William Mitchell, began to favour more chiselled looks, and that the image changed dramatically.

Before 1957, Cadillac rear wings had large tail-lamps with pressed steel bubbles surrounding them, but in 1957 the first of the large-finned cars appeared. In 1958 the fins were larger and the cars more bulbous (four-headlamp noses also became established), and for 1959 the height of the tail fins reached ridiculous proportions.

Then, slowly but surely, the fins began to be pared down as season followed season. The 1961 model had fins which swelled gently along the flanks from their origins on the big passenger doors. By 1963 the cars had become much more angular and slab-sided than ever, and for 1964 the fins remained only as a nostalgic reminder of the past. This was not only the last year of the fins, but also the last year of the Series 62 models.

In all these years, a Cadillac convertible was a very long car, running on a 129.5in/329cm wheelbase, and some cars weighed up to 4,700lb/2,128kg. They were all luxuriously, if somewhat garishly, equipped, all had very soft suspension which bucked and yawed on poor road surfaces, and there seemed to be power-assistance for every possible fitting. Body colours, naturally, were bright, and duo-tone treatments were often present.

A Cadillac-with-fins, in fact, represented everything that was good, and everything that was awful, about American motoring of the period. When the collectors' car boom hit the USA in the 1970s, it was inevitable that convertibles should become popular, and a well-preserved Cadillac became the most desirable of all.

OPPOSITE The birth, growth, and maturity of the Cadillac's fins – 1948 to 1961.

OPPOSITE, BELOW A 1955 Eldorado Brougham town car; note the extraordinarily aggressive bumper and the famous fins. Nothing succeeds like excess.

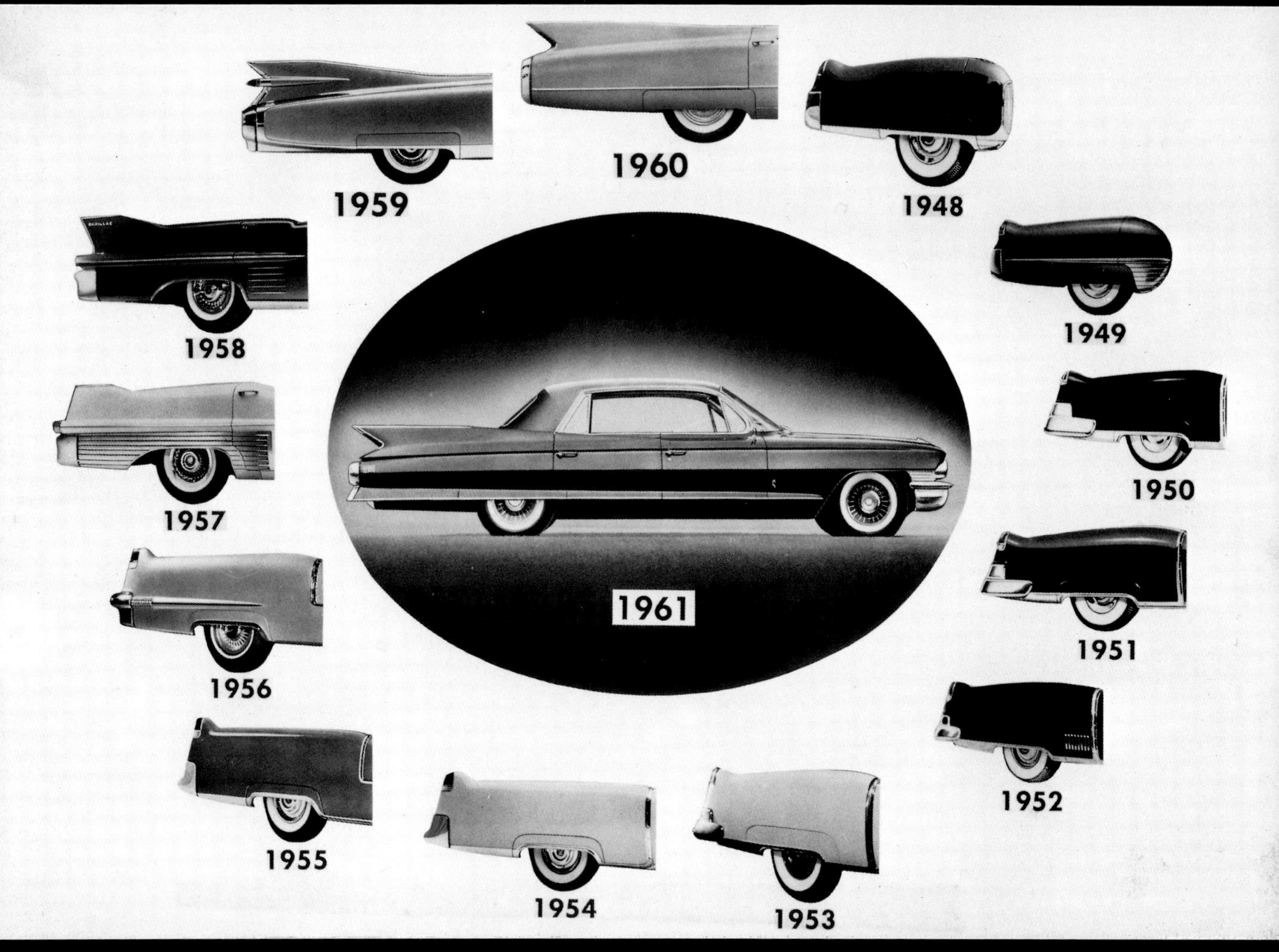
1959
1960
1948
1958
1949
1950
1957
1961
1951
1956
1952
1955
1954
1953

CADILLAC ELDORADO CONVERTIBLE

PRODUCTION SPAN
1970–1976

ENGINE
V8, ohv

CAPACITY
500 CID/8.2 litres

MAXIMUM POWER
190/235bhp

CHASSIS/SUSPENSION
Separate steel chassis frame, torsion bar and wishbone ifs, coil spring and radius arm beam rear

BODY STYLE
4 seater Convertible by Cadillac

TOP SPEED
115mph/185kph to 125mph/201kph, depending on engine

0-60MPH
10.0 seconds approx

In post-war years a Cadillac was, quite simply, the most prestigious of North American cars. For many years Cadillac's parent company, General Motors, allowed it to build a great variety of large six-seater saloons, convertibles, and limousines, all intended to be bigger, better-equipped, and more expensive than any domestic rival.

Then, in 1966, came the real break with tradition. Based on the general layout of the Oldsmobile Toronado, which had been announced a year earlier, Cadillac introduced its first ever front-wheel-drive car, the Eldorado Coupe. Compared with *any* previous Cadillac, the front-drive Eldorado was astonishingly different, advanced, and technically courageous.

It was asking a lot for a big car's front tyres to look after the steering, the braking *and* the driving of a car like this, but Cadillac's engineers had done a good job and, by Detroit standards, the Eldorado was very well-balanced.

It was definitely a car for the cognoscenti, for the advanced engineering was covered up by typical North American body styling. For the first few years the Eldorado was sold only as a closed coupe, but a convertible version was offered in 1971 and remained on sale for the next six seasons. In those years it was the only open- top car to carry a Cadillac badge, and sold steadily at the rate of 6,000 to 9,000 cars a year. It was finally killed off because of the safety implications of leaving passengers unprotected in roll-over accidents – and became an instant classic.

GM's particular solution to the front-drive packaging problem was to sit the big V8 engine above the line of the front wheels, to mount automatic transmission and final drive components alongside it, and to take the drive from engine to transmission through a massive and carefully developed chain. The separate chassis was really more of an elongated sub-frame, for its side members ended ahead of the rear suspension.

By the time the Eldorado convertible was launched, the car's style was almost indistinguishable from that of other Cadillacs. The car was extremely long (it rode on a 120in/305cm wheelbase at first, but on a 126.3in/321cm wheelbase after the first year), with large overhangs at front and rear. The bonnet had a proud and assertive prow, with a pair of headlamps tucked at each side of the rectangular grille, and the lines swept smoothly from nose to tail. The bonnet and the boot lid were both long, and the passenger accommodation thus came off second best. As the years passed, the style was slightly refined: 'opera' windows appeared in the hardtop version, and the grille style seemed to change every year.

The Eldorado was a car designed in the 1960s, now selling in the increasingly economy-conscious 1970s. By 1976, the last year in which an open-top version was available, an Eldorado weighed about 5,200lb/2,354kg, and would often record a single-figure fuel consumption. It was 'down-sized' for 1979, and lost much of its character.

OPPOSITE The last front- wheel-drive Eldorado convertibles were built in 1976, and still had the characteristic grille, and massive proportions of the earlier models. At the time, its loss was mourned, and such Caddys are now collectors' pieces.

1976

1976

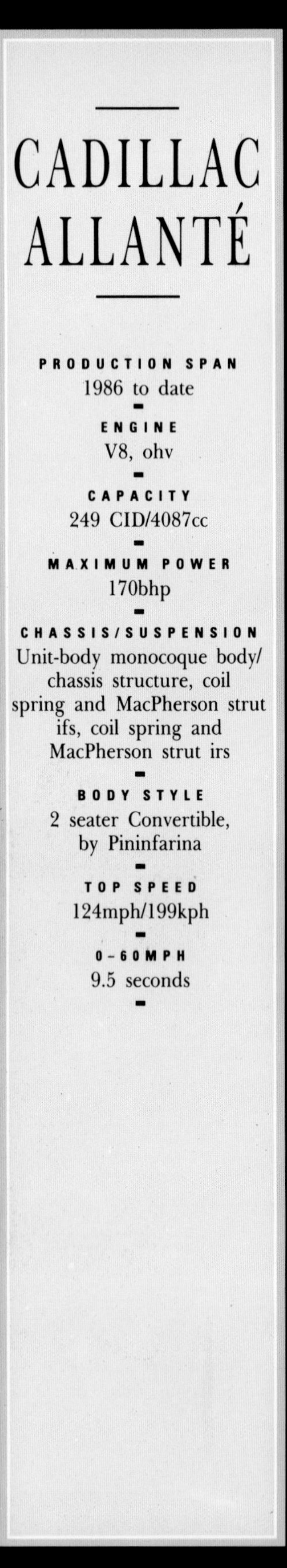

By the early 1980s, General Motors saw that it was missing out in one important market sector – the luxury sports-car market. In this exclusive sector of the motoring scene, those who habitually bought Gucci loafers and Armani shirts also seemed to buy Mercedes-Benz SL roadsters. GM, and Cadillac in particular, decided to do something about this.

For its new project, Cadillac approached Pininfarina of Italy, a distinguished styling house which it had known for many years. The deal which was eventually struck involved Pininfarina not only in the styling of a luxuriously equipped new two-seater sports car, but in developing and proving the structural engineering, and taking on the manufacture of the production shells. When the car was officially launched, Cadillac stated that it was organizing a regular 'air bridge' of painted and trimmed bodies from Italy to Detroit, three round trips a week, 56 bodies at a time.

Mechanically, the new car, called Allanté (the accent was considered a chic accessory) had a big, lazy, well-developed V8 engine, in a transversely positioned package, driving through a four-speed automatic transmission (there was no manual transmission alternative) to the front wheels. Front *and* rear suspension were independent.

This was effectively the same arrangement as used in several other contemporary Cadillacs, which meant that the exotically named Allanté was going to be easy enough to service in every part of North America.

It was the body style, of course, which was unique, and with a projected domestic price tag of $50,000 it needed to be as glossy, as distinctive, and as well-trimmed as possible. Even though the wheelbase was 99.4in/252.5cm, Cadillac provided only two seats, with a great deal of useful stowage space behind the leather-trimmed seats. Naturally there was electrical operation of almost everything – including soft-top erection, window lifts, seat positioning – and the car was so well equipped that the most significant equipment option was a cellular telephone.

Pininfarina produced a classic, if not outstandingly beautiful, body, which was clearly right for the sector it was aimed at. The drag coefficient, 0.34, was excellent for an open-top car, and it was the detailing of headlamp positions, spoilers and massive energy-absorbing bumpers that made this possible. The interior, of course, was mostly in carefully crafted leather, while the facia seemed to have more switches and controls than the average jet aircraft.

For those who could not stand the thought of a breeze in their carefully coiffured hair, Cadillac also offered a lift-off hardtop for the Allanté, which made the car look even more sleek than when it was open, and further reduced drag and fuel consumption. In so many ways – cast alloy wheel styles, general front end proportions and passenger accommodation – the Allanté was aimed at the Mercedes-Benz/Chrysler-Maserati sector. A bitter battle for sales will commence at the end of the 1980s.

OPPOSITE Ten years on from the Eldorado, Cadillac produced the smaller, more elegant, and Pininfarina-styled Allanté. It was still a fast car, but altogether more practical than the obsolete model.

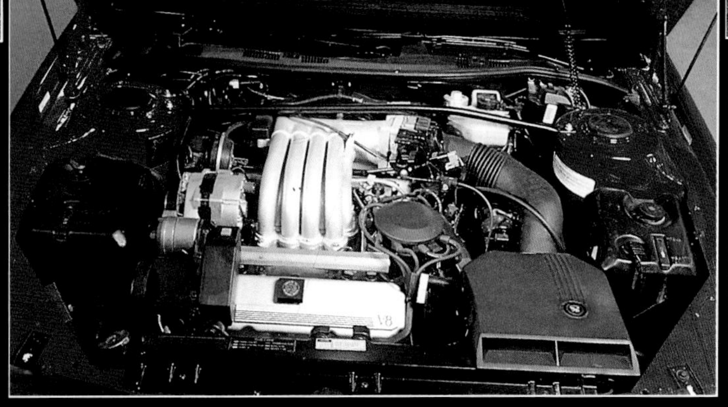

RIGHT The Allanté's engine bay houses a mass of plumbing, including a transversely mounted V8 engine driving the front wheels.

BELOW LEFT Pininfarina's problem with the Allanté, was that it had to marry style to practicability; there is no hiding those massive 'safety' bumpers.

CHEVROLET CORVETTE

PRODUCTION SPAN
1953–1962

ENGINE
6-cyl ohv, and V8 ohv

CAPACITY
235.5 CID/3.86 litres to 327 CID/5.36 litres

MAXIMUM POWER
150 to 360bhp, depending on engine

CHASSIS/SUSPENSION
Separate ladder-style chassis, coil spring and wishbone ifs, half-elliptic spring rear

BODY STYLE
2 seater Roadster, with lift-off hardtop option, by Chevrolet

TOP SPEED
107mph/172kph to 150mph/241kph, depending on engine

0-60MPH
11.0 to 6.0 seconds, depending on engine

The Chevrolet Corvette was the first two-seater sports car designed by General Motors, a company more famed for producing millions of flamboyant, but mundane, family saloons, hardtops and estate cars. The Corvette project began, in essence, as a Motorama 'one-off' show car in March 1953, but was speedily put into production.

The original Corvette production car was a rapidly, some say sketchily, developed machine, with a very basic chassis specification, a tuned-up version of Chevrolet's ubiquitous six-cylinder engine, and glass-fibre bodywork. When it became clear that the American sports car buff expected much more than this from the world's largest carmaker, development, modification and improvement began in earnest. By the early 1960s, when the next-generation Corvette (the first of the Sting Rays) was announced, the breed had been improved considerably.

From 1953 to 1962, all Corvettes were built on the same basic 102in/259cm wheelbase chassis, with rather floppy suspension. Six-cylinder engines were only used between 1953 and 1955. Chevrolet's new lightweight 'small-block' V8 engine was introduced in 1955, and was fitted to all cars from 1956 onwards. Original Corvettes were only built with automatic transmission, but a manual ('stick') option followed in 1956.

The original glass-fibre style, used until 1955, had two headlamps recessed in the front wings, a 'mouth-organ' grille, a wrap-around windscreen and detachable side-screens. For 1956 there was a completely new, larger, and more stylish body shell, with heavily sculpted sides behind the front arches, and wind-up windows; for the first time there was the option of a detachable hardtop with wrapped-round rear window. Fuel injection was offered in 1957.

The same basic body, modified to be 3in/7.6cm wider than before, and with four headlamps, was launched in 1958. This style was kept, with annual facelifts, until the end of the 1962 selling season. Every one had the severely wrapped-round windscreen and the dog-leg pillar feature which went with it. The vast majority had the fold-away soft top, but they looked smarter with the optional hardtop in place. To a whole generation of young Americans, if not to the rest of the world, this type of Corvette was the definitive open-top American car of the period.

It was not, of course, anything like the same kind of car as a European-style sports car such as a Jaguar or a Porsche. The accent was not only on form, but on embellishment and decoration, and whereas there was a good display of instruments in all these cars, there was also a great deal of glitz around them.

Even so, a well 'loaded' Corvette, with one of the very high-powered V8 engines which were optional, was a fast car by any standards, and some were equipped with fuel injection and aluminium cylinder heads. The attractiveness of the package is proven by the sales figures, which increased from 3,640 in 1954 to 14,531 in 1962.

RIGHT The original Corvette of 1953 evolved from the concept of a Motorama 'dream car', then progressively improved technically through the decade. From the beginning the body was built with glass-fibre mouldings, as on this 1954 model.

BELOW RIGHT High-style, Corvette-fashion . . . This was the instrument panel of the 1962 model.

CORVETTE

CHEVROLET CORVAIR MONZA SPYDER

PRODUCTION SPAN
1962–1964

ENGINE
Flat 6-cyl ohv

CAPACITY
145 CID/2.38 litres;
164 CID/2.69 litres

MAXIMUM POWER
150bhp

CHASSIS/SUSPENSION
Unit-body monocoque body/chassis structure, coil spring and wishbone ifs, coil spring and semi-trailing arm irs

BODY STYLE
4 seater Convertible, by Chevrolet

TOP SPEED
100mph/161kph

0-60MPH
10.0 seconds

In the late 1950s, each of North America's 'Big Three' – General Motors, Ford and Chrysler – designed a smaller and cheaper type of car, for the 'Compact' category. Those from Ford and Chrysler were strictly conventional, but the GM design, the Chevrolet Corvair, was technically adventurous.

By any previous North American standards, the Corvair was different, for GM's designers had obviously been studying the VW Beetle phenomenon. Not only did the Corvair have a rear-mounted engine, but this was an air-cooled unit with a flat-six layout. Because of the location of the engine, the Corvair had a preponderance of weight in the tail, and strong oversteering tendencies. The motoring press greeted the new car with incredulity, and interest; it went on to have a controversial and stormy career.

The basic style of the Corvair became known as 'inverted bathtub', because of the pronounced crease all around the waist of the various body styles. Most Corvairs had saloon, estate-car or sometimes coupe versions of this style, all on the same 108in/274cm wheelbase, but from the autumn of 1961 a more powerful version known as the 'Monza', sold either as a coupe, or an even more graceful Spyder, was put on sale.

This car, even though it only sold at the rate of 10,000 a year at first, soon developed a cult all of its own, particularly as it was powered by an early example of that 1980s phenomenon, the turbocharged engine. The engine, like others with a similar configuration, had a very distinctive exhaust note, which added to the model's distinctive character.

Monza Spyders were considerably faster than other Corvairs, had multi-instrument facia panels, and a number of other sports and handling accessories all built in to the standard specification, and they were certainly more spacious than the alternative imported sports cars of the period.

The two factors militating against success for the Monza Spyder were cost – $500, nearly a quarter more than that of a normal-engined Coupe – and quirky, somewhat 'nervous', handling. At this time the Corvair was under attack from the consumers' friend, Ralph Nader, and there is no doubt that the adverse publicity harmed sales even though the Spyder was not an evil-handling car at all.

The Monza of this period, in fact, had very similar 'family' styling to other and larger Chevrolets, but it was a much less decorated car than its larger relatives. Because Corvair sales in general were on a downward trend at this time, the turbocharged Monza Spyder was not the success that it might have been; when the completely re-engineered 1965 Corvair appeared, the Monza Spyder was dropped.

RIGHT The Corvair Monza Spyder of 1962 was the world's first production car to use a turbocharged engine. Technology was still somewhat crude, but the effect was magnificent.

BELOW Compared with the rather Plain- Jane saloon, the Corvair Spyder was a smart and neatly-proportioned four-seater soft-top model. The proportions were so carefully worked out that there is really no hint of a rear-engine position.

CHRYSLER-MASERATI

PRODUCTION SPAN
1986 to date

ENGINE
4-cyl ohc/2 ohc

CAPACITY
135 CID/2213cc

MAXIMUM POWER
174/205bhp

CHASSIS/SUSPENSION
Unit-body monocoque body/chassis structure, coil spring and MacPherson strut ifs, coil spring and radius arm rear beam

BODY STYLE
2+2 seater Convertible, by DeTomaso/Maserati

TOP SPEED
124mph/199kph; 137mph/220kph

0-60MPH
Not known

The industrial scene can sometimes change rapidly. In the late 1970s, Chrysler and Maserati were both in major financial difficulties, yet by the mid-1980s both were healthy and active once again. Better still – the two companies had joined forces to produce a new and luxurious car, the Chrysler-Maserati.

The link-up, originally, was a personal one, for Chrysler's boss Lee Iacocca, and Maserati's owner Alejandro DeTomaso had first done business together when Iacocca was at Ford, on the DeTomaso Pantera project. Once Iacocca and his team had rescued Chrysler from oblivion, it was natural that a similar image-building project should be considered.

The Chrysler-Maserati was a car designed in Detroit – mechanically *and* in its styling – with Maserati charged with the design of the interior, and also with responsibility for assembly of the production car. The basis of the design was Chrysler's familiar transverse engine/transmission front-wheel-drive package, as used in models like the Le Baron and New Yorker family cars, this time mounted in a specially designed steel monocoque with a 93in/236cm wheelbase.

The new car, which was clearly aimed at the Mercedes-Benz SL market, was a smoothly detailed two-door convertible, having 2+2 seating. Like all the latest wind-cheating styles, this was a very integrated shape, with wrap-around headlamp/turn indicator units and a small grille in the nose, matched by a full-width, but slim, display of lamps at the rear. The body was surprisingly long, at 176in/447cm, for a car with such a compact wheelbase, but this ensured a very large boot, even if there was not enough space for four seats. Maserati's interior style featured soft-tuck leather, and achieved a very 'European' ambience.

Each Chrysler-Maserati was to be sold as a full convertible, with power-operated soft top, along with the provision of a lift-off hardtop. The soft top was beautifully tailored, while the smooth hardtop featured portholes in the rear quarters of the type once seen in two-seater Thunderbirds, and in other American cars of the 1970s.

The car's engine was not, as some had hoped, from Maserati, but was a further-developed version of Chrysler's own 2.2-litre/135 CID unit. There were two versions, both with turbocharging; the more powerful unit had a 16-valve cylinder head and twin overhead camshafts, and produced no less than 205bhp. Without a doubt, this was the most exciting Chrysler engine for many years. Five-speed manual, or three-speed automatic, transmissions were available.

In the late 1980s, the category which this car was to contest is positively overcrowded, for the Cadillac Allanté and the latest Mercedes-Benz models are all trying to attract the same customers.

ABOVE Two famous names were brought together in 1986 with the launch of the Chrysler-Maserati convertible. The running gear, and the style, were by Chrysler of Detroit, with Maserati looking after the interior design and final assembly.

LEFT Like every fashionable mid-1980s car, the Chrysler-Maserati had a low nose and a high tail. The engine was transversely mounted, and drove the front wheels.

CITROEN DS

CABRIOLET

PRODUCTION SPAN
1961–1971

ENGINE
4-cyl ohv

CAPACITY
117 CID/1911cc;
133 CID/2175cc

MAXIMUM POWER
78/106bhp

CHASSIS/SUSPENSION
Unit-body monocoque body/chassis structure, hydro-pneumatic suspension and leading arm ifs, hydro-pneumatic suspension and trailing arm irs, with self-levelling

BODY STYLE
4 seater Cabriolet, by Henri Chapron

TOP SPEED
93mph/150kph;
107mph/172kph

0-60MPH
21.2/14.4 seconds

In 1934, Citroen took a giant leap ahead of the rest of Europe by introducing its first rakish front-wheel-drive car. Then, after the Second World War, it introduced that lovable 'chicken-coop', the 2CV. Thereafter, it was always obvious that Citroen stood for advanced engineering. The futuristic DS19 of 1955 merely confirmed this.

Except that it had used an old engine design, Citroen's DS19 was a machine of exciting specifications. Not only did it have a wind-cheating styling which was far ahead of its time (and of economic necessity) and front-wheel-drive, but it had all-independent self-levelling suspension by high-pressure hydro-pneumatic units, four-wheel disc brakes and full-power steering, in each case with power generated by a pump on the hard-working engine.

At first, there is no doubt, the DS (or 'Goddess', as it soon became known in France) was underpowered, but Citroen gradually rectified this, and from 1965 also introduced more powerful units for the DS21 and its descendants.

Citroen itself concentrated on the building of four-door saloons and lengthy five-door estate cars. In 1959, however, the French coachbuilder, Henri Chapron, showed a convertible version of the DS19 at the Paris Salon, and a year later this had officially been adopted by Citroen. Deliveries began in 1961, and were to continue for ten years. Some extremely special, lengthened, versions, were supplied to the French government.

Chapron's *décapotable* (which is French for 'convertible') was no more and no less than a thorough conversion of the existing DS saloon, which in any case had much of its structural strength in its underside. Ahead of the windscreen, and below the waistline, the styling of the convertible was the same as that of the saloon; it was all so neatly done that some people failed to notice that there were two passenger doors instead of four!

The Chapron Cabriolet kept all of the Citroen's idiosyncratic mechanical features, including the one-spoke steering wheel, the strange transmission, and of course the astounding self-levelling suspension. There was the same shark-like nose and (at first) the prominent headlamps at the front of each wing. The doors, naturally, were much longer than those normally fitted at the front of a Citroen, so as to allow access to the rear seats. The soft top, when erect, fitted neatly around the wind-up windows, but most people agreed that a Chapron Citroen looked smartest of all with the soft top furled and stowed away under a neat cover. Some cars were fitted with detachable hardtops.

Over the years, the Cabriolet's equipment changed along with that of the saloon, the most obvious visual change coming in the autumn of 1967 when a lower four-headlamp nose was adopted, in which one pair of lamps was connected to the steering, and swivelled when the wheels turned. Demand for the costly Chapron car finally died away when the faster and more specialized Citroen SM C...

ABOVE Simple Gallic identification – the twin Chevrons denote a Citroen, and DS21 the model type.

OPPOSITE With its Cabriolet top furled, the Chapron-style Citroen was a smart open-air machine. The saloon's long wheelbase was retained, and there was still ample room for four occupants.

OPPOSITE, BELOW Years before the rest of the world discovered aerodynamic styling, Citroen was practising the art of air-flow management. Launched in 1955, the 'basking shark' style of the Citroen DS was still efficient in the 1970s.

DATSUN (NISSAN) 280ZX T-BAR

PRODUCTION SPAN
1979–1983

ENGINE
6-cyl, ohc

CAPACITY
168 CID/2753cc

MAXIMUM POWER
140/145/180bhp

CHASSIS/SUSPENSION
Unit-construction steel body/chassis structure, coil spring and MacPherson strut ifs, coil spring and semi-trailing arm irs

BODY STYLE
2+2 seater T-Bar type Coupe/Spider, by Nissan

TOP SPEED
112mph/180kph, or 129mph/208kph with 180bhp engine

0-60MPH
9.8/7.4 seconds

Although the Japanese motor industry expanded mightily in the 1950s and 1960s, it was some time before companies like Toyota and Datsun found time, and interest, to begin designing sports cars. Datsun's original efforts were only partly successful, but the 'Z-Car' types which followed were world-beaters.

The original 240Z made its debut in 1969, a combination of established Datsun engineering and dramatic styling inspired by the German designer Albrecht Goertz. Its looks featured a long sharp nose, and a fastback coupe cabin, and in character (with a six-cylinder overhead cam engine) was like that of the recently obsolete Austin-Healey 3000.

Not only was there a choice of engines for different markets, but also a choice of names – some were Nissans, some were Datsuns, some were Fairlady Zs, while others had no 'Fairlady' in the title.

As so often happens with cars like this, the first idea was the best, and the purest, of all. The later, larger-engined 260Z and 280Z types were less sporting and heavier, but with less responsive engines – yet the public still loved them.

The second-generation Z-Car was the 280ZX, which was launched in 1978. Although this retained the 280Z's engine, it was a larger and altogether more Americanized style, with different rear suspension and more interior space. As with the later 260Z/280Z models, there was a choice of two-seater or 2+2 seater, but both cars were closed coupes at first.

Then, from the end of 1979, the 280ZX 2+2 T-Bar model was announced. This car, as you might expect, looked almost exactly like the coupes, but had two removable smoked-glass panels in the roof, one on each side of a permanently fixed central buttress linking the screen rail to the rear roll hoop, to form the reinforced 'T-Bar'.

Before long the T-Bar model was accounting for half of all 280ZX sales, so it could certainly be counted a success. All the cars in this range had long and flowing lines, with recessed (though exposed) headlamps, massive bumpers designed to look after USA legislative requirements, a large glass hatchback, and well-trimmed interiors usually featuring cloth-covered seats. As you might expect of a car intended to sell well in the USA, automatic transmission was an option, as was full air-conditioning.

Complaints that the 280ZX had lost its edge compared with the early cars were met, in 1981, by the launch of a 180bhp turbocharged version. This car was 25 per cent more costly than normal aspirated examples and was only ever sold in North America.

The Japanese, it must be admitted, never lost sight of their main objective, which was to dominate the mid-size sports coupe market in the USA, and with a whole series of Z-Cars they certainly achieved this. There was no harm, it seemed, in making a Japanese car with many American-style features – the 280ZX's successor, the V6 powered 300ZX, was even more 'trans-Pacific' than ever.

ABOVE By the early 1980s Nissan offered a Z-Car with all possible features, including the new-fangled T-Bar roof, and a 180 bhp turbocharged engined. It was aimed directly at the USA market and was a great success.

DETAIL 1 LEFT In the Good Old Days, such recessed lamps would have been covered by fairings, but modern regulations put a stop to that.

DETAIL 2 BELOW LEFT Functional styling included louvres to let out hot under- bonnet air, and a NACA duct to urge fresh air into the turbocharger ducting.

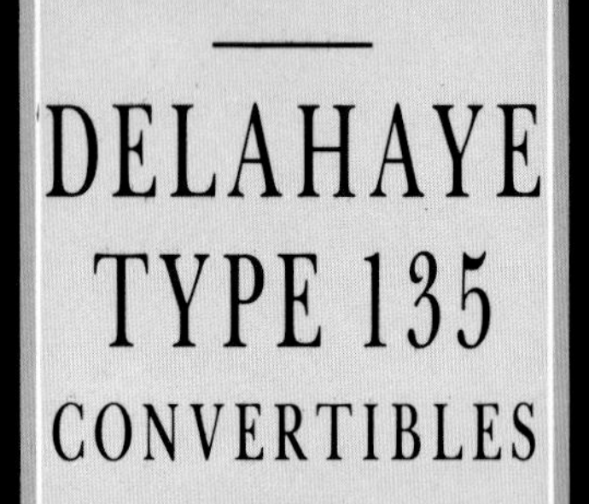

DELAHAYE TYPE 135 CONVERTIBLES

PRODUCTION SPAN
1934–1950

ENGINE
6-cyl ohv

CAPACITY
198 CID/3237cc;
217 CID/3557cc

MAXIMUM POWER
130/160bhp

CHASSIS/SUSPENSION
Separate steel chassis frame, transverse leaf springs and wishbone ifs, half-elliptic leaf spring beam rear

BODY STYLE
4 seater bodies, including Convertibles by specialist coachbuilders

TOP SPEED
(Typical 130bhp machine)
95mph/153kph

0-60MPH
(Typical 130bhp machine)
13.7 seconds

Delahaye was a famous French company which started by building brick-making machinery, and turned to cars in 1895. Throughout the 'vintage' period, Delahaye made dull but dependable cars, and it was not until 1933 that a prototype of the much faster and more excitingly specified Type 135 range was shown.

The Type 135's sporting and *Grand Routier* character was all the more surprising when one considers the origins of the engine. This, although a powerful, rugged and surprisingly efficient overhead-valve six-cylinder unit, was a development of that already used in the company's commercial vehicles. For the new car, however, it was linked to a new synchromesh gearbox, or alternatively to the French Cotal electro-magnetic transmission, and from 1936 it was offered in a yet more powerful guise, with 160bhp at 4,200rpm for competition purposes. That, incidentally, was the equal of what Jaguar would claim, for its new XK engine, 12 years later . . . .

Not only was the Type 135 the fastest Delahaye ever produced, but it also had a thoroughly modern chassis. At a time when many large and fast cars still relied on beam axle front suspension, the latest Delahaye used coil spring independent front suspension, and this helped the outright sports-racing versions of the car to be competitive.

The new car's wheelbase was a generous 116in/295cm, so it was an amply spacious chassis onto which a whole variety of specialist coachwork could be fitted. Delahaye produced its own standard styles – saloons, coupes and tourers – but many were also fitted with luscious special bodies of the type which only the French were building at this time.

Perhaps these cars, many of them sleek sports saloons, drop-head coupes or lightweight sports tourers, did not quite have the restrained elegance of a Hispano-Suiza or a Rolls-Royce, but they were seen to be absolutely right for the 'smart set' who regularly rushed up and down the arrow-straight *Routes Nationales* between Paris and the Riviera.

Although some cars retained free-standing headlamps, many had contoured fronts, no running boards and sharply swept tails. It was not only the French styles, but the names of the coachbuilders themselves – Latourneur et Marchand, Henri Chapron, Henri Labournette et Cie, and above all Figoni et Falaschi – which typified the romance of the period.

These Delahayes were wonderful examples of the way that a style can belong to an era. In the late 1930s, when the rich refused to admit that another war might be imminent, they were a perfect statement of attitude by an entire social stratum. After the Second World War, even though the Type 135 was re-introduced and built in small numbers for a few years, it looked all wrong for a country where much of the countryside was devastated. The best of these cars, for sure, were the late 1930s models.

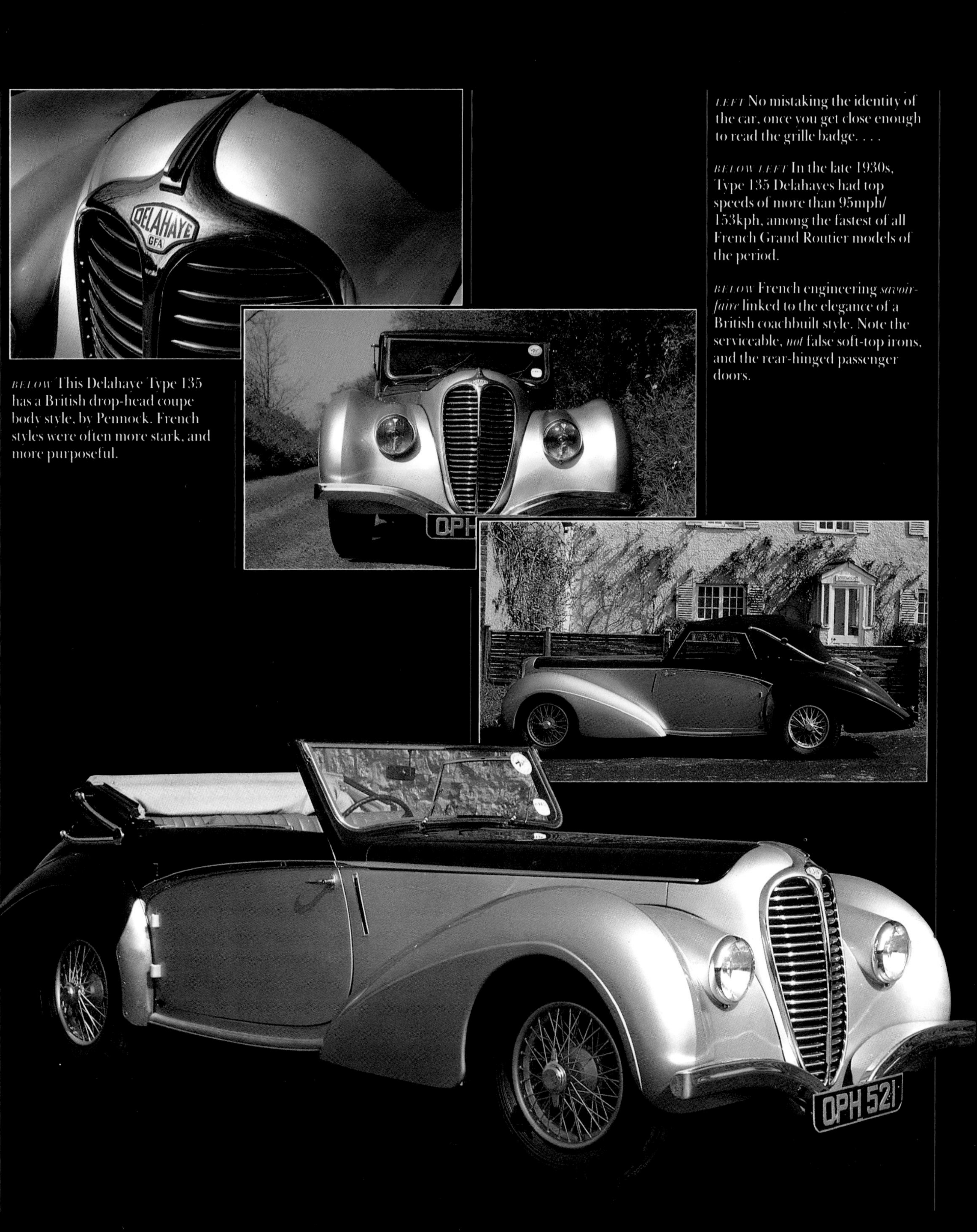

LEFT No mistaking the identity of the car, once you get close enough to read the grille badge. . . .

BELOW LEFT In the late 1930s, Type 135 Delahayes had top speeds of more than 95mph/ 153kph, among the fastest of all French Grand Routier models of the period.

BELOW French engineering *savoir-faire* linked to the elegance of a British coachbuilt style. Note the serviceable, *not* false soft-top irons, and the rear-hinged passenger doors.

BELOW This Delahaye Type 135 has a British drop-head coupe body style, by Pennock. French styles were often more stark, and more purposeful.

DUESENBERG J & SJ CONVERTIBLES

PRODUCTION SPAN
1928–1937

ENGINE
8-cyl 2 ohc

CAPACITY
420 CID/6882cc

MAXIMUM POWER
200/320/400bhp

CHASSIS/SUSPENSION
Separate steel chassis frame, half-elliptic leaf springs front beam, half-elliptic leaf spring and radius arm beam rear

BODY STYLE
2 seater and 4 seater bodies, including Convertibles by specialist coachbuilders

TOP SPEED
Up to 135mph/217kph, depending on engine

0-60MPH
Down to 10.0 seconds, depending on engine

Because they were designed without an eye to cost, the Model J and SJ Duesenbergs were the most magnificently engineered US cars of the inter-war period. It was, and is, a lasting miracle that such an expensive and flamboyant motor car could continue to be sold through the depths of the Depression. Most of these cars have survived to this day.

This car, the undisputed 'King of the Classics', was engineered by Fred Duesenberg, whose company was owned by E. L. Cord. Cord's brief to him was simple – he wanted it to be the best-engineered, and the fastest, car in the world. Cord wanted to be able to sell a car which was as magnificent as a Bugatti Royale, and as well-regarded as a Rolls-Royce. Duesenberg therefore evolved a brand-new and quite peerless engine, in a conventional chassis with a choice of long – and extremely long – wheelbases (142.5in/362cm or 153.5in/390cm).

The previous Duesenberg (Model A) engine had been advanced enough, so the new unit had to be exceptional. Fred Duesenberg therefore created a 6.9-litre/420 CID, twin-overhead-cam, four-valves-per-cylinder colossus, which produced 200bhp in its most basic form, and 320bhp in SJ (S=Supercharged) form. Even the 'basic' Model J could beat 110mph/177kph, and the SJ was good for more than 120 or even 125mph/201kph.

Bodies, by the very best of American coachbuilders, were stunning, and quite unmatched by any other car maker. And so they should have been: in 1928 when the car was announced, a Model J chassis *alone* cost $8,500 (this rose to $9,500 from 1932), while average 'ready to roll' prices were around $15,000 – at least double that asked for a current V16-engined Cadillac.

A typical coachbuilt Duesenberg shell had a proud radiator which looked uncannily similar to that of a 'W.O.' Bentley, and carried twin spare wheels in pouches in the flowing wings above and behind the front wheels themselves. Wire-spoke wheels were normal wear, and the bonnets were so regally long and so high that it helped to be a tall driver.

Some cars had saloon (sedan) bodies, but many had beautifully equipped drop-head coupe bodywork. At this price, of course, Duesenberg was happy to provide any sort of body that its rich and exclusive customers demanded. Some had dickey-seats and cramped main passenger compartments, some had full-length open-top styles, and a handful had rakish roadster styles.

The American film stars Clark Gable and Gary Cooper took delivery of short-chassis SSJs, with roadster bodies. Thirty-six SJs were sold, and near the end of the production run there were a few Model JNs, but the original-type Model Js were the most numerous. All in all, 470 cars were produced in nine years, and it was the financial collapse of E. L. Cord's empire which finally killed off these fabulous creations.

OPPOSITE The early 1930s Duesenbergs – this was a 1933 Speedster – were as magnificent as any motor car so far built in the USA, and faster than any other car in the world.

INSET, OPPOSITE Every detail of the Duesenbergs was meant to indicate power, style, and wealth. Can one detect a touch of W.O. Bentley in the radiator shape?

OVERLEAF The age of conspicuous consumption! Does it matter that this huge eight-cylinder twin-cam engined car only had two seats? Its character said everything about its creators – E. L. Cord and Fred Duesenberg – and about its first owner.

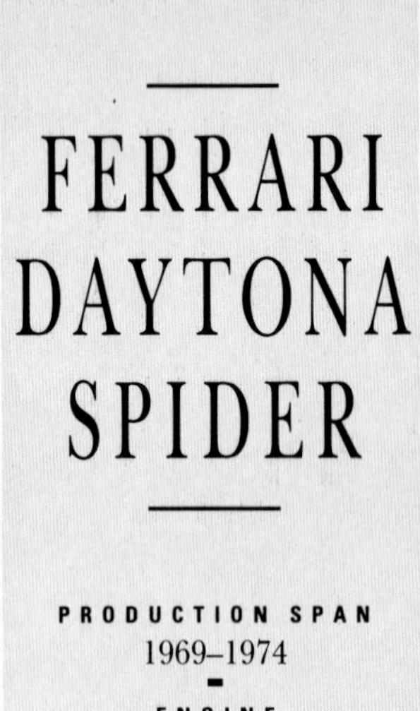

FERRARI DAYTONA SPIDER

PRODUCTION SPAN
1969–1974

ENGINE
V12, 2 ohc

CAPACITY
268 CID/4390cc

MAXIMUM POWER
352bhp

CHASSIS/SUSPENSION
Separate multi-tubular chassis frame, coil spring and wishbone ifs, coil spring and wishbone irs

BODY STYLE
2 seater Convertible, by Scaglietti

TOP SPEED
174mph/280kph

0-60MPH
5.4 seconds

Ferrari built a series of stunning front-engined supercars in the 1960s, but none was more outstanding than the definitive example, the famous Daytona. Like most of Ferrari's two-seaters, this was conceived as a fixed-head coupe, but a Convertible (or, as the Italians usually describe it, a 'Spider') was developed later.

The Daytona's chassis was a development of that originally designed for the 275GTB model of 1964. This was the first ever Ferrari road car to have independent suspension at front *and* rear, and it was also distinguished by the use of a front-mounted V12 engine and a combined gearbox/final drive transaxle at the rear.

The first 275GTBs had single-cam V12s, the later cars twin-cam units, but the Daytona chassis which followed not only had a twin-cam V12, but a much larger one – 4.4-litres/268 CID, with no less than 352bhp. Like the late-model 275GTBs, engine and transaxle were rigidly tied together by a large-diameter torque tube.

The Daytona's body style, by Pininfarina, was simply stated and gorgeous; the car had a long and low nose, originally with headlamps hidden behind a transparent panel, a sharply raked windscreen and a smoothly tapering roof over the two seats. Luggage space was limited. The coupe itself was announced in the autumn of 1968, and like all Ferraris of the period the bodies were produced in quantity by Scaglietti in Modena.

The launch of an open-top version was inevitable, and the prototype actually appeared at the Frankfurt Motor Show of September 1969. Few modifications were needed for Pininfarina to convert the coupe to a convertible, the open-topped car retaining the same screen, the same doors and winding windows, and the same general proportions, including the straight-through crease along the flanks. Cars sold in the USA always had a different type of nose in which pop-up headlamps were used, and this feature spread to cars built for all other markets by 1971.

The Daytona not only looked magnificent, but had astonishing performance, roadholding and character. Though the Spider version might not have had quite as high a top speed as the coupe, the Daytona was one of the fastest front-engined road cars ever built, which speaks volumes for its aerodynamic efficiency.

It was an enthralling experience to drive around behind the splendid V12 engine, which was at once very powerful and very docile, beautiful to look at *and* made all the right sort of urgent tappety noises that a Ferrari buff desires. A Daytona Spider, soft top down, was the ideal sort of car for a rich man to use for cruising along sun-drenched highways.

It was, however, the last of its kind, for the front-engined Daytona was eventually displaced by the mid-engined Boxer, which was only ever sold as a closed car.

LEFT Some Ferrari styling themes were carried on, lightly modified and improved, from model to model, and there was always Pininfarina's detailing to hold it all together. The Daytona's front end featured turn indicators, parking lights, bumpers and sheet metal in a delicately sculpted whole.

BELOW For many this was the ultimate Ferrari convertible – for the 365GTS/4 was the last front-engined Ferrari V12 which also offered open-top motoring. The GTS was much more rare than the fastback GTB/4 – and today it is much more valuable. Have a look at the styling, consider the performance, and surely you can see why.

FERRARI DINO 246GTS

PRODUCTION SPAN
1972–1973

ENGINE
V6, 2 ohc

CAPACITY
148 CID/2418cc

MAXIMUM POWER
195bhp

CHASSIS/SUSPENSION
Separate multi-tubular chassis frame, coil spring and wishbone ifs, coil spring and wishbone irs

BODY STYLE
2 seater Convertible, by Scaglietti

TOP SPEED
148mph/238kph

0-60MPH
7.1 seconds

The first mid-engined Ferraris were all racing cars – single-seaters or sports prototypes – and the evolution of a road car followed on from that. The first sports-racing Dino (the name is that of Enzo Ferrari's only son, who died in 1956) appeared in the 1960s, using a completely new design of twin-cam V6 engine, and it was a later development of this engine which was also chosen for the road cars.

The first prototype coupe was shown in 1965, with the engine longitudinally mounted behind the two seats. The production car, which looked the same and was at first called the 206GT, had a light-alloy 2.0-litre/121 CID engine which was transversely mounted and drove the rear wheels through a combined gearbox/transaxle.

In 1969 the 206GT was replaced by the 246GT, which had an enlarged iron-block V6 engine, and a slightly longer wheelbase, but the style and engineering were otherwise identical. This was the chassis used until 1973, and for the last two years there was also an open-top version, the 246GTS.

Both cars used the same type of multi-tubular chassis frame, in which the passengers sat well forward. The waistline was so low that Pininfarina had to shape large wheel arch bulges over the fat tyres, the result being a sensuous little car which sold very well indeed.

Because of its mechanical layout – the engine/transmission pack was tucked in very close behind the seats – the 246GTS could not be a full convertible. Instead, Ferrari, in conjunction with Pininfarina, copied Porsche's 'Targa' idea, merely giving the car a removable roof panel, and the option of stretching a soft top – between the screen rail and the rigid bodywork behind the seats – to keep out the rain.

The Dino, whether sold as a coupe or a spider, broke new ground for Ferrari in many ways. Most important of all was that it was not *officially* a Ferrari at all, but a Dino, for the cars were not sold with Ferrari badges. This fiction, encouraged by Enzo himself to preserve the memory of his son, didn't last long with Ferrari enthusiasts, many of whom added Ferrari badges, and all of whom called the car a Ferrari anyway!

Not only that, but the Dino was the first V6-engined Ferrari road car, and the first to use a mid-engined layout. It was also the smallest-engined Ferrari for many years, as all previous road cars had been V12 monsters, some with 4.4-litre/268 CID or even 4.9-litre/303 CID displacement.

In many ways, therefore, this was the 'budget' price Ferrari (if such a thing was possible!), aimed squarely at the Porsche 911 market. With rather more attention to quality control, and with a bigger dealer network, it would have sold even better – even so it was the best-selling Ferrari so far put on sale. After the 246 range was dropped in favour of the new V8-engined cars, the famous V6 engine/transmission pack also found a home in Lancia's enormously successful Stratos competition car.

OPPOSITE The Dino's engine had an impeccable pedigree designed by Jano for racing, productionized and produced in numbers for Fiat, and used to power Ferrari and Fiat Dinos. The V6 engine had four overhead camshafts, produced plenty of torque and power, and made the most exquisite noises. From any angle, the Ferrari Dino was a gorgeous little two seater; no-one could fault the Pininfarina lines. The Spider version kept almost all of the same lines as the coupe; the only 'open-top' area was above the seats.

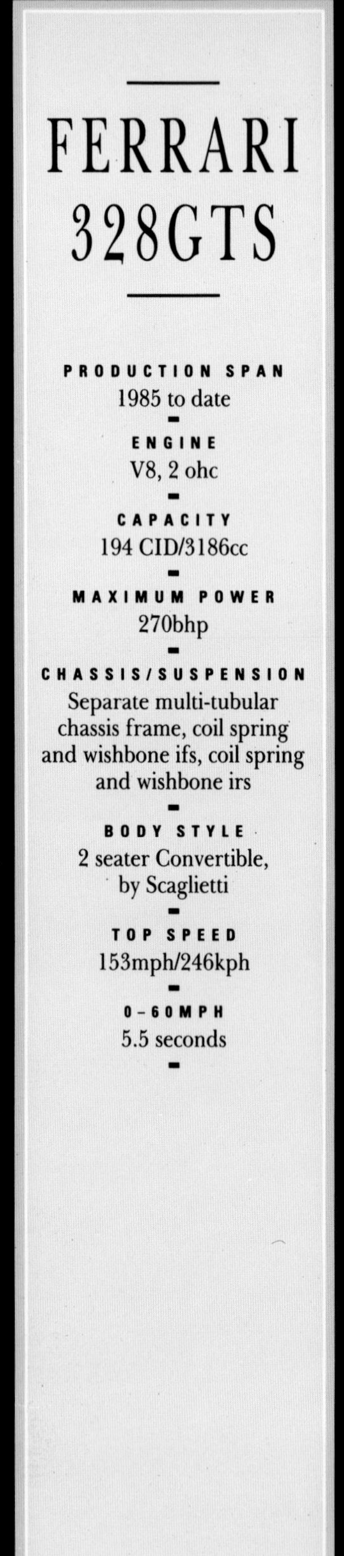

FERRARI 328GTS

PRODUCTION SPAN
1985 to date

ENGINE
V8, 2 ohc

CAPACITY
194 CID/3186cc

MAXIMUM POWER
270bhp

CHASSIS/SUSPENSION
Separate multi-tubular chassis frame, coil spring and wishbone ifs, coil spring and wishbone irs

BODY STYLE
2 seater Convertible, by Scaglietti

TOP SPEED
153mph/246kph

0-60MPH
5.5 seconds

To replace its successful V6-engined Dino series, Ferrari decided to retain the same basic mid-engined chassis layout, but to produce a new engine. Starting in 1973, therefore, the 246GT engine was replaced by the 308GT unit, a powerful new 2.9-litre/179 CID V8 engine.

Within two years Ferrari were selling Bertone-bodied 2+2 seaters, and Pininfarina-styled two-seater coupes, the latter known as the 308GTB. Two years later, in 1977, the 308GTS Spider, effectively the successor to the open-topped Dino 246GTS Spider, was also launched. Except that the Bertone car was eventually replaced by the Pininfarina-styled 2+2 Mondial in 1980, this range of V8-engined Ferraris continued in production into the late 1980s.

Ferrari had to fight hard to keep its cars abreast of USA exhaust emission laws, one result being that the V8 engine was given fuel injection in 1980, and heads with four valves per cylinder in 1982. The next important change, phased in from the autumn of 1985, was that the engine was enlarged to 3186cc/194.5 CID. The result of all these changes was that 12 years after the original 308GT engine was announced, the engine had grown, and was just 15bhp and 15lb ft of torque sharper than before.

Pininfarina's 308GTB/GTS style was acknowledged as an all-time-classic shape, right from the start. By the late 1980s it had still not been necessary to change a single major panel because the Americans, in particular, loved it just as much as they had done in the mid-1970s.

In many ways the 308GTB/GTS was merely a refinement of the previous generation 246GT/GTS type, with less pronounced wheel arch bulges, and slightly more angular lines around the tail. Ducts into the engine bay, positioned ahead of the rear wheels, were fed by air along the flanks through sculptured channels in the door pressings, while there was a low and wide nose channeling air into the front-mounted radiator. At the rear, the tail was sharply cut off, very much after the style of the legendary Daytona. The sail panels linking roof to rear quarters were arguably more elegantly treated than those of the Jaguar XJ-S.

As with the earlier Dino, the GTS Spider was really no more than a GTB with a removable roof panel; the screen and the rear quarter styling were retained for both cars. The GTS, like the GTB, had wind-up windows and even with the top removed was a draught-free car at very high cruising speeds.

The 308/328 V8 engine was as powerful, sounded just as exciting, and was as reliable as any other Ferrari unit. It was originally the first engine from Maranello to use cogged belt drive for its camshafts.

By the late 1980s, even though it was not available with four-wheel drive, anti-lock brakes or other high-tech developments, the 328GTS was still seen as one of the world's most desirable open-top machines. A successor, when it came, would have to be truly outstanding.

RIGHT The 308-328 series of Ferrari used the same basic chassis as the Dino of 1967-1973, but were fitted with a newly designed 90-degree V8. Styling, need it be said, was by Pininfarina, another timeless shape built in both coupe and convertible types.

ABOVE The 308/328GTC models were extremely popular in the United States – in California especially – but were less common in Europe.

LEFT Ferrari's 90-degree four-cam V8, launched in 1973, was the very first V8 to be sold by the Italian company. It originally had two valves per cylinder, but by the early 1980s it had been given four-valve heads and fuel injection.

FIAT 1500/1600 CABRIOLET

PRODUCTION SPAN
1959–1966

ENGINE
4-cyl, ohv or 2 ohc

CAPACITY
75 CID/1221cc;
90 CID/1481cc;
91 CID/1491cc;
96CID/1568cc

MAXIMUM POWER
58/72/80/90bhp

CHASSIS/SUSPENSION
Unit-construction steel body/chassis structure, coil spring and wishbone ifs, half-elliptic leaf spring rear

BODY STYLE
2 seater Cabriolet, by Fiat

TOP SPEED
90mph/145kph to 105mph/169kph, depending on engine

0-60MPH
19.1 to 10 seconds, depending on engine

Although Fiat was Italy's most important car manufacturer, it did not seriously begin to develop sports cars until the 1950s. Its first attempt, the Trasformabile of the mid-1950s, was a rather ungainly machine, and it was not until 1959, with the Pininfarina-styled Cabriolets, that it found the correct balance.

During the 1950s, Fiat had introduced a new range of 1.1-litre/66.5 CID saloon cars, with a good, though conventional, chassis, and a sporting reputation in its 1100TV form. The unsuccessful Trasformabile had used that car's underpan and running gear, and so did the next generation of Cabriolets. The new car also had an exciting new engine option with which to boost its image, the OSCA-designed twin-cam unit.

The new-generation Cabriolet was previewed in 1958, but did not actually go on sale until 1959, and initially it was sold with a 1.2-litre/74.5 CID pushrod Fiat engine, and a specially designed 1.5-litre/91 CID twin-cam alternative which the specialist company of OSCA had designed. The model family then remained in production for seven years, and along the way the pushrod engine was exchanged for a new 1.5-litre/90 CID type in 1963. The OSCA unit was slightly enlarged in the autumn of 1962.

The twin-cam cars gained front-wheel disc brakes from 1960, the pushrod-engined cars gained front discs in 1963 at the same time as the twin-cam cars gained *four*-wheel discs, and a new five-speed gearbox was fitted from 1965.

The Cabriolet's smart body, built in steel at the Pininfarina factory, was based on the pressed-steel underpan and most of the running gear of the existing 1100/1200 saloon's monocoque. Compared with the lumpy Trasformabile, the new Cabriolet had smooth lines with a characteristic front grille, uncluttered sides, neat tail-lamps on the rear corners and wind-up windows in the doors. Like most contemporary Italian sporting cars, the Cabriolet had a lot of painted metal in evidence inside the cockpit, with the instruments grouped ahead of the driver's eyes.

Because the twin-cam cars cost considerably more than the Fiat-engined cars, those fitted with Fiat's own mass-production four-cylinder units were much more numerous than those with the OSCA engines; but it was the OSCA-engined cars which made most headlines, and figured in most road tests.

Although the Fiat Cabriolets sold much faster than the Trasformabile had done, they would eventually be overshadowed by the 124 Sport Spiders which took over (at Pininfarina and at Fiat) from 1966. They were, nevertheless, the foundation upon which the 124 Spider's success was based.

ABOVE Except that it has been fitted with non-standard wide-rim wheels, this Fiat Cabriolet looks as smart as the day it was built, in the early 1960s.

OPPOSITE Pininfarina produced a simple, but exquisite, body style for the Fiat Cabriolets of the early 1960s. The same shape covered three distinctly different engines in seven years.

OPPOSITE, BELOW LEFT This Cabriolet interior, which dates from the early 1960s, was typical of Italian style of the period, with a neat instrument display, but much painted metal to back it all.

OPPOSITE, BELOW RIGHT The pushrod ohv engine of this Fiat Cabriolet is well hidden by an air cleaner. The most exciting versions had twin-cam units designed for Fiat by OSCA.

FIAT DINO SPIDER

PRODUCTION SPAN
1966–1973

ENGINE
V6, 2 ohc

CAPACITY
121 CID/1987cc;
148 CID/2418cc

MAXIMUM POWER
160/180bhp

CHASSIS/SUSPENSION
Unit-construction steel body/chassis structure, coil spring and wishbone ifs, half-elliptic leaf spring and radius arm rear (2000), coil spring and semi-trailing arm irs (2400)

BODY STYLE
2+2 seater Spider, by Pininfarina

TOP SPEED
127mph/204kph;
130mph/209kph

0-60MPH
8 seconds

In the mid-1960s, Ferrari wanted to build racing cars for the new F2 regulations, and chose his existing V6 Dino engine to power them. New rules, however, required 500 engines to be built, and Ferrari had never done this before. Enter a Fairy Godmother, the Fiat organization.

Not only did Enzo Ferrari persuade Fiat to 'productionize' his V6 engine, but to use it in a new Fiat sports car, and along the way he also secured supplies for use in the confusingly named Ferrari Dino sports car. The two types were in production throughout the same period, but were entirely different in layout.

Fiat sponsored the production of two front-engined Dinos – a long-wheelbase four-seater fastback coupe, with bodies styled and produced by Bertone, and a short-wheelbase 2+2 seater open-top Spider, styled and produced by Pininfarina. Both these coachbuilders had their factories in Turin, as did Fiat; Fiat supplied underpans to each coachbuilder, who completed the bodies and sent them back to the Fiat factory for final assembly.

The Pininfarina Spider made its debut at the Turin Motor Show in November 1966. It used the light-alloy 2.0-litre/121 CID version of the engine, a modified Fiat 2300 gearbox, and was equipped with a solid rear axle, single-leaf springs and radius arm rear suspension. Three years later the car was thoroughly redesigned, though not re-styled, with the iron-block 2.4-litre/148 CID V6 engine, a ZF gearbox and coil spring independent rear suspension taken from the brand-new Fiat 130 executive saloon.

The Spider rode on an 89.8in/228cm wheelbase, and had a deliciously chic open-top body style. There were pronounced curves over and around the wheels (which were the same as those to be used on Ferrari's mid-engined Dino sports car), and the front was low and wide, with four circular headlamps. The tail was sharply cut off, resembling other designs that Pininfarina had produced for Ferrari.

Even though it was an out-and-out sports car, the Fiat Dino had a spacious 2+2 cockpit (although the rear was best used as an upholstered luggage stowage area), with ample weather protection including deep body sides and wind-up windows. The facia display was full of instruments, and the rev counter's red warning sector only began at 7,200rpm. Sensational . . . .

The front-engined Dino's most outstanding feature was its urgent character, for it had an engine that positively crackled with power and flaunted its sporting heritage; even in its original, perhaps under-developed, form the Spider had excellent roadholding and a great deal of performance. The Bertone-bodied coupe, being longer and heavier, felt different – yet it easily outsold the Spider, which tells us a lot about the worldwide trends of the late 1960s/early 1970s.

Although the original Fiat Dino was assembled at Fiat, the last 2.4-litre cars were assembled at the newly extended Ferrari factory at Maranello.

RIGHT This was the Pininfarina-styled short-wheelbase Dino Spider, with curvaceous lines, and 2+2 seating.

RLJ 976R

RLJ 976R

LEFT Not a straight line in sight: from any viewpoint the Pininfarina-styled Dino Spider is a curvaceous beauty.

BELOW LEFT The Fiat Dino's style is unmistakable, even if the owner has customized it – there should be a Fiat badge on the nose, but no Ferrari prancing horse on the grille.

LEFT There's no doubt what sort of engine is fitted to this Fiat Dino, for the speedometer reads to 155mph/250kph, and the rev-counter red-line is set at 8,000rpm.

BELOW Two types of Dino were built concurrently, in Italy: this was the front-engined car produced by Fiat, but with Pininfarina body styling. The Ferrari badge on the tail is an owner fitment.

FIAT X1/9

PRODUCTION SPAN
1972 to date

ENGINE
4-cyl, ohc

CAPACITY
79 CID/1290cc;
91 CID/1498cc

MAXIMUM POWER
75/85bhp

CHASSIS/SUSPENSION
Unit-construction steel body/chassis structure, coil spring and MacPherson strut ifs, coil spring and MacPherson strut irs

BODY STYLE
2 seater 'Targa' type Coupe/Spider, by Bertone

TOP SPEED
99mph/159kph;
106mph/171kph

0-60MPH
12.7/11.0 seconds

Although it was not the world's first mid-engined production car, Fiat's X1/9 was still a trend-setter in 1972. Not only was it elegant, nippy, practical and with an appealing character, but it was a great advance on established sports-car design standards. That it was absolutely 'right' from the day it was put on sale is proved by its production figures, still healthy in the late 1980s.

Bertone originally conceived this beautiful little transverse mid-engined two-seater as a possible replacement for the 1960s-style Fiat 850 Spider, and it was soon adopted by Fiat. For the first decade, Bertone of Turin manufactured, painted and trimmed the structures, with final assembly at Fiat, but after that Bertone took over the complete assembly process, and the car theoretically became a 'Bertone' and not a 'Fiat'.

The key to the design was the engine location. In 1969 Fiat had introduced the all-new 128 hatchback, which had a transversely mounted overhead-camshaft engine at the front, and front-wheel drive. For the new sports car, Fiat simply used the entire 128 engine/transmission/final drive assembly, in 128 Rally tune, and re-positioned it behind the seats, driving the rear wheels. 128-type MacPherson strut suspension was used at the front, similar modified components at the rear, and the whole was tucked into a very neatly packaged two-seater structure.

Not only was the X1/9 beautifully and crisply detailed, with a wedge nose, a removable roof panel (which could be stowed and carried in the front luggage compartment if desired) and an additional luggage box in the tail, but there were many other practical features. The petrol tank, for instance, was tucked away behind one seat, and the spare wheel behind another – the spare having to be extracted through the cockpit in the event of a 'flat'.

The original car had rather 'bitty' bumper details, but these were cleaned up (if made a trifle larger) later in the car's career. Some X1/9s had steel disc wheels, while others sported smart cast-alloy wheels. All had a styling crease along the flanks and a black plastic cover over the engine bay. Like the original Porsche 'Targa', the car looked as smart, and was almost as windproof, with the roof panel off as with it on.

Although the X1/9 was a better car in every respect than the MG Midget or the Triumph Spitfire, it was by no means a fast car. From 1972 to 1978 it had a 75bhp engine, and a top speed of less than 100mph/161kph. It was only from 1979 onwards, when the engine had been enlarged to 91 CID/1499cc and a five-speed transmission had been fitted, that it became a genuine 100mph car. Unhappily, Fiat seemed to lose interest in the X1/9 from the early 1980s, and although the car was kept abreast of legislative requirements, it received no further development, and no further improvement. An X1/9 of the late 1980s is no better, no faster and no more fuel-efficient than the original X1/9-1500 of 1979.

RIGHT The Bertone style for the X1/9 survived into the late 1980s. This is a Bertone-badged model, produced after Fiat handed over the whole project to the Italian coachbuilding concern.

BELOW RIGHT X1/9 styling is so neat that it is difficult to spot the mid-engine mounting. This is the 1500 5-speed model, with the bigger front and rear bumpers, and the raised engine lid.

X1/9

FORD THUNDERBIRD 2-SEATER

PRODUCTION SPAN
1954–1957

ENGINE
V8, ohv

CAPACITY
256 CID/4.19 litres;
292 CID/4.78 litres;
312 CID/5.11 litres

MAXIMUM POWER
160 to 340bhp, depending on tune

CHASSIS/SUSPENSION
Separate chassis frame, coil spring and wishbone front, half-elliptic spring and beam rear

BODY STYLE
2 seater Convertible, by Ford

TOP SPEED
(Typical: 225bhp)
113mph/182kph

0-60MPH
(Typical: 225bhp)
10.2 seconds

For some years after the Second World War, Ford-USA concentrated on building hundreds of thousands of large, reliable family cars. It was only after Ford's rival, General Motors, unexpectedly put the two-seater Chevrolet Corvette on sale, that Ford was inspired to react; the famous Thunderbird two-seater was the result.

Like the Corvette which preceded it, and the Mustang which was to follow in the 1960s, the Thunderbird was a stylish new sporting car which drew heavily on existing corporate parts already used in other models. The Thunderbird, however, had a new 102in/259cm wheelbase chassis frame, allied to a smart new body style which, in the American fashion of the day, had barrel sides, a 'straight-through' wing line from headlight to tail-lamp cluster, and a fully wrapped-round windscreen with a pronounced 'dog-leg' pillar. Detachable spats covered the rear wheels, and there were styled air vents in the tops of the front wings and on the bonnet panel. Unlike most European sports cars, the Thunderbird had a bench seat.

Although the running gear came from other Fords, with several different overhead valve V8 engine options, and with a choice of manual or automatic transmissions, the styling was at once different and refreshingly crisp. All these first-generation Thunderbirds were two-seater convertibles with capacious boot accommodation, and there was a detachable hardtop available as an option. This top, which turned the car into a wind- and waterproof two-seater saloon, was plain-panelled at first, but from 1956 there was the option of circular portholes in the rear quarters. 1955 models had spare wheels in the boot area, but for 1956 this was placed outside in front of the rear bumper, aping the Lincoln Continental Mark I which was already such a legend in American motoring history.

Ford, of course, wanted to see their new Thunderbird annihilate the Corvette, and in sales terms it certainly did; they would also have liked to kill off the imported sports cars from Europe. The new Ford, however, was too large (it weighed more than 3,000lb/1,360kg) and too softly sprung to behave like a European sports car, although it was also a fast car with a great deal of charm.

Even though the Thunderbird was outselling the Corvette by a factor of four to one, Ford management was determined to drive it upmarket and make it larger when the time came for a restyle. The second-generation Thunderbird of 1957 ran on a much longer, 113in/287cm wheelbase and was a full four-seater. Nor was the replacement car a sports car, but something which Ford called a 'personal' machine. This, together with the more obvious charms of the 1955–1957 variety, explains why a two-seater Thunderbird became a collector's piece in the 1970s, when auto nostalgia was at its height.

RIGHT Latter-day enthusiasts can always identify a late-model two seater Thunderbird by the 'porthole' option in the detachable hardtop. This became available in 1956, but just to confuse those enthusiasts, some earlier cars were treated to the porthole top by their proud owners.

BELOW RIGHT The last of the two-seater Thunderbirds was built in 1957, after which Ford produced a much larger, less sporty four seater. The '57 typified the love of glitz which marks that period, though the fins, thank goodness, never reached excessive heights.

Thunderbird

FORD FAIRLANE 500 SKYLINER

PRODUCTION SPAN
1956–1959

ENGINE
V8, ohv

CAPACITY
272 CID/4.46 litres to 352 CID/5.77 litres

MAXIMUM POWER
190 to 300bhp

CHASSIS/SUSPENSION
Separate chassis frame, coil spring and wishbone front, half-elliptic spring and beam rear

BODY STYLE
5 seater Hardtop/ Convertible, by Ford

TOP SPEED
90mph/145kph to 110mph/177kph, depending on engine

0-60MPH
15 to 10 seconds, depending on engine

For many years there was a Fairlane in Ford-USA's model lineup, a popular 'full-size' range of cars which in almost every case followed the accepted design convention of the day. By the mid-1950s this meant that a Fairlane was a roomy five/six-seater with lots of power, sloppy roadholding and a long list of optional extras. All cars of this type were sold as saloons, convertibles, estate cars and sometimes as pick-up trucks.

Then, in 1956, Ford astonished the motoring establishment by unveiling the Skyliner, which had a body style never before attempted (and never copied since). In short, this could look like a conventional two-door hardtop saloon – except that at the touch of a button it could turn itself into a fully open convertible. This, incidentally, was achieved while retaining the normal exterior style of a late-1950s Fairlane, and without help from advanced electronics.

The Skyliner was the only example of the retractable hardtop roof ever put on sale. When the roof was unclipped from the screen rail and the electro-hydraulic mechanism was then activated, the large boot lid opened up (it was hinged at the rear, rather than at the front), the roof neatly folded down its front few inches, after which the whole top retracted into its hiding place in the boot. The boot lid then closed, and the transformation was complete.

It was an astonishing offering which, unhappily, could embarrass its owner if any of the sequence-controlled mechanism misbehaved. There was also the inescapable problem that, with the roof retracted. there was very little stowage space of any kind, which was ludicrous for a car measuring about 210in/533cm from stem to stern. At a time when Fairlanes cost about $2,600, the extra cost of $400 for the unique retracting roof style deterred many customers, yet more than 47,000 were produced.

In all other respects, the Skyliner was just a conventional Ford of the period, which is to say that it had a separate chassis frame, with soft, long travel, suspension, the accent being on a good 'town' ride rather than firm balance at high speeds. The brakes, frankly, were poor – but so were they on other American cars of the period.

Up front there was a wuffly and dead-reliable V8 engine, usually matched to an automatic transmission. Many had 'comfort' options including electric seat adjustment, electric drop windows, a radio (not standard in those days) and much more.

Ford styling, at this time, was at its most expansive, with a wide-mouth front grille, swooping chrome 'wing' lines along the sides and rear wings which changed from sharp in 1957 to bulbous and rather more muted in the next two seasons. The windscreen had a strong 'dog-leg' feature, and there were bench seats at front and rear.

All in all, this was a fascinating car, a unique offering which could only have been born out of blasé confidence. As one historian later commented, it was 'a reminder of an age when Detroit thought it could do anything'.

RIGHT The roof was hinged so that it rose, then moved backwards, as the furling process continued.

BELOW RIGHT The Skyliner's front corner style was so typical of the period – heavily sculptured and decorated.

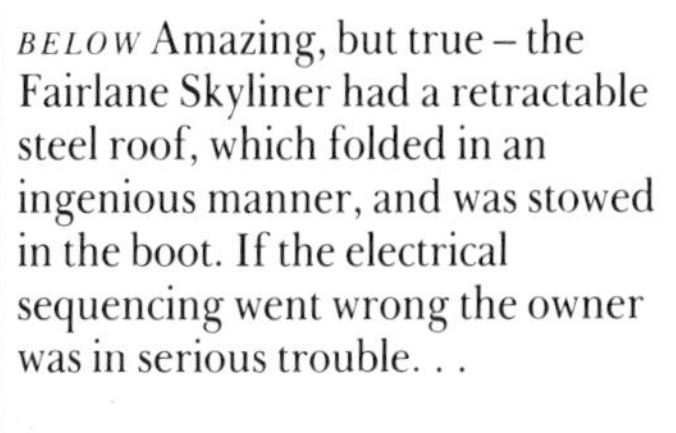

BELOW Amazing, but true – the Fairlane Skyliner had a retractable steel roof, which folded in an ingenious manner, and was stowed in the boot. If the electrical sequencing went wrong the owner was in serious trouble. . .

FORD MUSTANG

PRODUCTION SPAN
1964–1973

ENGINE
6-cyl, ohv, and V8, ohv

CAPACITY
170 CID/2.78 litres to 429 CID/7.02 litres

MAXIMUM POWER
98 to 375bhp

CHASSIS/SUSPENSION
Unit-construction body/chassis structure, coil spring and wishbone front, half-elliptic spring and beam rear

BODY STYLE
5 seater Convertible, by Ford

TOP SPEED
100mph/161kph to 125mph/201kph, depending on engine

0-60MPH
12.5 seconds to 6 seconds, depending on engine

Without much doubt, the Mustang was the single most famous Ford car introduced in the USA after the Second World War. Conceived in the early 1960s, and put on sale in 1964, it broke every sales record in the book over the next few years. It inspired Ford's main competitor, General Motors, to develop rivals, with Chrysler and American Motors eventually following suit. Ford of Europe were to draw heavily on Mustang experience when designing the Capri.

Lee Iacocca, now sometimes known as 'the father of the Mustang', saw the need for a simple, relatively small, but fast and sporty car to sell to the growing number of young drivers. Except for the limited-production Chevrolet Corvette, he reasoned, there was no domestic sporty car in the USA; the new car could fill a yawning gap.

And so it did. By American standards, not only was the Mustang cheap and cheerful, but it was sold in an astonishing number of versions. The meekest of all had six-cylinder engines, the most extrovert had vast, rumbling, gas-guzzling V8s. Some had hardtop bodies, some were fastbacks and a great number were convertibles. All of them had four-seater accommodation.

The Mustang was quick and easy to develop because it drew all its running gear from Ford's corporate 'parts bin'. The dreary Falcon, in particular, was a principal source, but the biggest and most powerful V8s came from the largest Fords then being built or planned.

Only the unit-construction body styles were unique, and had to be specially developed. The first Mustang rode on a 108in/274cm wheelbase, but this was stretched by an inch (2.5cm) for 1971. Lengths gradually crept up from 181.6in/461cm in 1964, to 189.5in/481cm for 1971. The original 1964 style was re-skinned for 1967; there was another re-style for 1970, and this model became the largest Mustang of all for the 1971–1973 period.

Each of these cars remained faithful to the long bonnet/short tail style of the original, though at each facelift the shell became smoother, the lines sleeker, and the tail higher and looking somehow more bulky. All of them were two-door models with wind-up windows. The convertibles looked much better when new, and when the soft tops fitted properly; somehow, there was nothing quite so tacky as a beaten-up Mustang convertible which had been neglected.

All the most desirable Mustangs had large-capacity V8 engines, 'four on the floor' (a four-speed manual gearbox with floor-mounted change speed lever), fat tyres and all manner of dress-up kits. Limited production types, such as the super-tuned Shelby GT350/GT500 models, and cars fitted with 'Boss' or 'Mach 1' engines, were even more popular in later life than they had been when new.

The Mustang was a car which was absolutely right for the 1960s, but not for the economy-conscious era which followed. The Mustang II which took over for 1974 was a much smaller, slower and less exciting car altogether.

LEFT By the early 1970s the original Mustang concept had been lost. The car had become bigger, leaner, but not faster. It was, nevertheless, a very attractive soft-top indeed.

BELOW The original Mustang, launched in 1964, caused a sensation. It was sold in convertible, hardtop and, eventually, in fastback guise. Today's collectors choose the convertible every time.

JAGUAR XK120

PRODUCTION SPAN
1948–1954

ENGINE
6-cyl, 2 ohc

CAPACITY
210 CID/3442cc

MAXIMUM POWER
160/180bhp

CHASSIS/SUSPENSION
Ladder-style chassis frame with cruciform, torsion bar ifs, elliptic leaf spring rear

BODY STYLE
2 seater Roadster or Drop-head Coupe, by Jaguar

TOP SPEED
120mph/193kph

0-60MPH
10 seconds

William Lyons began his business career in Blackpool, with a company building special bodies for motorcycle sidecars. It was a natural progression to produce special bodies for cars, then to launch the SS car, and finally to produce the SS-Jaguar in 1935.

During the Second World War, Mr. Lyons not only planned a series of new models, but an exciting family of twin-cam engines to power them; these were called XK units, and were to be built in Coventry for the next 38 years. Although he had wanted the first new model to be a saloon car, post-war tooling bottlenecks got in the way, and the very first XK-engined car to meet its public was the XK120 sports car of 1948. It was at that time the fastest production sports car in the world.

In the drab, post-war, car-starved world of 1948, the beautifully styled XK120 caused a real sensation, and although Jaguar had intended to produce it only in limited numbers, those plans were soon expanded, and from 1950 the 160bhp two-seater was available in larger quantities. Many of the cars were sold in the USA, thus founding the Jaguar cult which has persisted to this day.

The XK120 was new from end to end, with torsion bar independent front suspension on a 102in/259cm wheelbase, the extremely powerful and very impressive-looking engine, and of course its remarkable looks. Not only did these cars look wonderful, but they were extremely fast *and* they seemed to make all the right noises.

All previous Jaguars had used 1930s-type looks, with long flowing wings, running boards under the doors and free-standing headlamps, but the new XK120 was much more 'continental' in its looks, with full-width styling, curvaceous but graceful flanks and a narrow front grille with the headlamps tucked away at each side.

The original XK120 was sold only as a two-seater Roadster, and had aluminium bodywork built up on a wooden framework, but from 1950 a new and fully tooled pressed-steel shell took its place; the actual styling was not changed. This car had a simple foldaway soft top which sat rather high over the vee-screen, and there were removable side curtains on the cutaway doors. A neat fixed-head coupe version followed in 1950, but it was not until April 1953 that the extremely well-equipped drop-head coupe appeared. This car had a tailored and padded soft top with a fully fitted interior, and there were different doors, with opening quarter windows and wind-up glass.

The XK120, of course, was only the first of three different XK production models, for in 1954 the XK120 was replaced by the more powerful, better-handling and even better-equipped XK140, which looked almost the same as before, while in 1957 the XK150 was a rather more matronly derivative of the style, with a curved single-piece screen, but still on the original chassis. The last of the XK sports cars was built in the winter of 1960/1961, and its even more memorable successor was the E-Type.

OPPOSITE, LEFT By the early 1950s, the original XK120 Roadster had been joined by the very smart, and well-trimmed, Drop-Head Coupe.

OPPOSITE, CENTRE The coupe still lacked the rear bumper protection which American buyers needed.

OPPOSITE, RIGHT In spite of its flashing performance, and graceful exterior style, the XK120 Drop-Head Coupe retained a traditional British type of wooden facia, with a four-spoke steering wheel, and wind-up door windows.

OPPOSITE, BELOW The front-end detail of all XK120s was exquisite, with not a straight line in sight. Later XKs took their inspiration from this layout too.

SPP 192

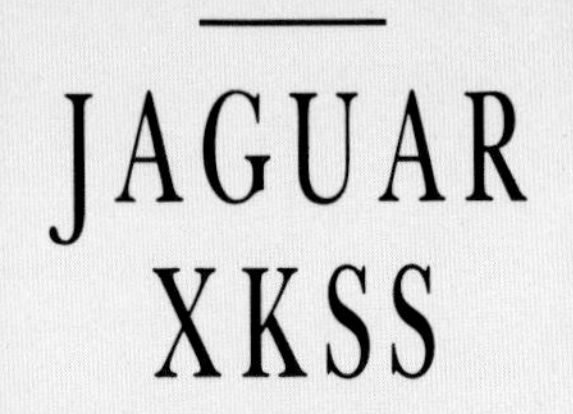

JAGUAR XKSS

PRODUCTION SPAN
1957 only

ENGINE
6-cyl, 2 ohc

CAPACITY
210 CID/3442cc

MAXIMUM POWER
250bhp

CHASSIS/SUSPENSION
Unit-body centre section, with multi-tubular front and centre frame, torsion bar ifs, torsion bar and trailing link rear

BODY STYLE
2 seater Roadster, by Jaguar

TOP SPEED
144mph/232kph

0-60MPH
6.0 seconds

Jaguar's famous and very rare XKSS – only 16 cars were built – became legendary although it was a marketing failure. It was, in any case, a car developed to 'use up' a stock of D-Type racing sports cars, and even then it took a long time to sell the small number produced. Perhaps it was a blessing that a factory fire put a stop to the possibility of building any more.

Jaguar, having launched the famous twin-cam XK engine in 1948, soon got involved in sports-car racing, first with modified XK120s, and from 1951 with the specially developed XK120C, or C-Type, competition car. Then, in 1954, Jaguar produced the racing D-Type, initially as a 'works' racing car, and from 1955 as a limited-production machine for worldwide sale.

Unhappily for Jaguar, more D-Types were built than could be sold, so at the end of 1956 a bold decision was taken – the unsold stock of D-Types would be lightly reworked, and sold as 'road-going' cars called XKSS. There was no question of these race-proved and very starkly equipped machines being de-tuned – they were merely given better weather protection, a bit more passenger space and a new image.

The D-Type had been built around a wind-cheating oval-shaped cross section, with the two seats demanded by international regulations, but very limited leg room for the 'passenger' who, if carried, had no screen ahead of him, for there was only a piece of perspex wrapped around the driver's side, and a headrest behind his head.

For the XKSS conversion, which was not really intended as a road car, but as a machine for use in USA 'production-car' racing, the D-Type was given a full-width curved windscreen, the headrest and the metal spine between the body seat cut-outs were removed, a second door was added to the left side and fixed sidescreens were added to those very steeply contoured but tiny doors. Smart (though functionally insignificant) bumpers were added at front and rear, a luggage rack was fixed to the top of the tail and a fold-down soft top was also added. Because the entire front end was hinged at the nose, there was excellent access to the engine bay and front suspension for maintenance work.

All this turned the D-Type into a rather more habitable machine, but there were still many 'race only' features – no heating, no stowage space inside the car, and a fuel filler hidden *inside* the soft top, which therefore had to be folded down before the car could be re-fuelled in wet weather! The so-called silencer was still no more than a gesture to regulations, and the overall effect was of an ultra-rapid Supercar which could be used on the public highway if its rich owner was so inclined.

The XKSS, like the D-Type, looked beautiful because of its elegant and well-curved styling. Most of the running gear was adapted from that used in Jaguar road cars, and this explains why so many 'replica' cars of this most charismatic machine have been constructed in recent years.

CENTRE, TOP When Jaguar converted D-Types into XKSS 'road cars', it discarded the hump behind the driver's head, added a full-width screen, and a fold-down soft top.

CENTRE, MIDDLE The XKSS, like the D-Type from which it was derived, had a magnificent 250bhp version of the six-cylinder XK engine, complete with three Weber twin-choke carburettors.

CENTRE, BELOW 'The office' of the XKSS was slightly more civilised than that of the D-Type, but still had restricted leg room, and virtually nowhere to stow anything. But with all that performance in reserve, no-one seemed to care. . . .

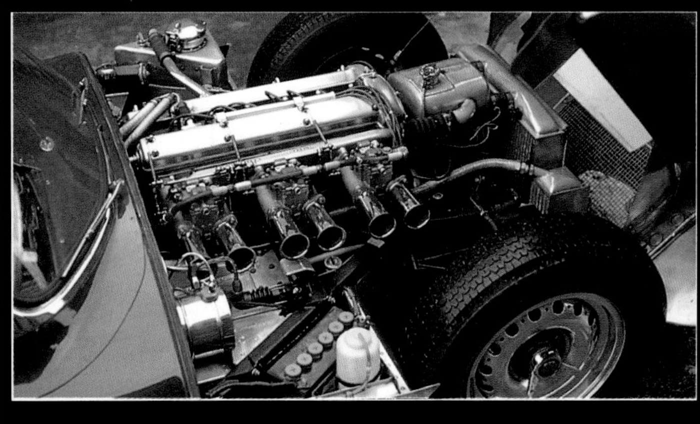

BELOW Jaguar's rare, and exclusive, XKSS, was no more than a road-equipped version of the D-Type racing sports car. For road use, however, the car was given a full-width wrap-around screen, side-curtains for the doors, and a rather flimsy-looking bumper.

JAGUAR E-TYPE

PRODUCTION SPAN
1961–1975

ENGINE
6-cyl, 2 ohc, and V12, ohc

CAPACITY
230 CID/3781cc;
258 CID/4235cc;
326 CID/5343cc

MAXIMUM POWER
265bhp/272bhp

CHASSIS/SUSPENSION
Unit-body centre section, with multi-tubular front frame, torsion bar ifs, coil spring wishbone and fixed-length drive shaft irs

BODY STYLE
2 seater Roadster or Coupe, or 2+2 Coupe, by Jaguar

TOP SPEED
150mph/241kph
(146mph/235kph for V12)

0-60MPH
7.0 seconds
(6.5 seconds for V12)

Jaguar built the XK family of sports cars for more than 12 years. In that time, technology had advanced apace, and so had Jaguar's thinking. In place of the conventional XK models, Jaguar introduced the sexily styled E-Type, which made headlines all round the world.

A new car, always coded E-Type, was actually conceived in 1956, to succeed the D-Type as a racing sports car, but following Jaguar's withdrawal from motor racing, the new model became 'softer', better-equipped, and altogether more civilized. Originally meant to be only an open two-seater, it was also developed as a fastback/hatchback coupe. Even if some of the management team doubted that it would sell in large enough quantities, it was prepared for production and put on sale in 1961.

Original E-Types had 3.8-litre/231 CID six-cylinder engines, but for 1965 the unit was enlarged to 4.2-litres/258 CID. Then, in 1971, the E-Type became the first Jaguar to use the brand-new 5.3-litre/326 CID V12 engine, a unit which had still not reached the peak of its development in the late 1980s. Every time a more powerful engine was made available, legislative changes (particularly in the USA) obliged Jaguar to de-tune once again. The result is that the V12 was really very little faster than an original 3.8-litre, though it was better developed, and more versatile.

Structurally, and in its styling, the E-Type was a further evolution of the D-Type/XKSS layout, with a monocoque centre section, a multi-tubular front end and the same sleek and flowing lines which were never successfully copied by any other car maker. Like the mid-1950s D-Type before it, the first E-Types had headlamps tucked away behind transparent covers, as well as high and rounded tails and rather minimal two-seater accommodation.

Demand for soft-top roadsters and fixed-head types was almost equally matched. The fixed-head model was arguably better styled, and had more, and certainly more useful, luggage accommodation. The Roadster, on the other hand, still had wind-up windows in its doors and a full-size curved screen, plus a folding soft top which clung to its job even at the very high speeds of which an E-Type was capable. From 1966, too, there was a longer-wheelbase version of the fixed-head car, which had extra occasional seats, and was predictably called the '2+2' model.

A well-maintained E-Type not only looked marvellous, and had the same sort of appearance as a limited-production Italian Supercar, but it also had excellent handling and brakes *and* its engine was so docile that it could be trickled gently around town, or up and down the boulevards of Los Angeles, without losing its composure.

Above all, however, it was the E-Type's styling, the feline grace of its lines and the animal-like purr, or throb, of its excellent engine which made it such an exciting proposition. When it was eventually dropped in 1975, the world of motoring grieved – and the car which took over, the XJ-S, was not at all the same type of machine.

OPPOSITE, INSET In the 1960s, the Jaguar E-Type became one of the most easily-recognized cars in the world.

RIGHT After ten years, Jaguar redesigned the E-Type, turning it into Series III with a brand new V12 engine. From this point, all types were built on the longer wheelbase underframe.

RIGHT, BELOW All E-Types had curvaceous rears, with the exhaust system taking a prominent part in the style.

FAR RIGHT, BELOW E-Type facias were comprehensively equipped. Naturally the big speedometer and rev-counter dials were placed ahead of the driver's eyes.

676 EWV

12 MY

JAGUAR XJ-S CABRIOLET

PRODUCTION SPAN
1983 to date
(no 6-cyl engine for 1988)

ENGINE
6-cyl, 2 ohc, and V12, ohc

CAPACITY
219 CID/3590cc;
326 CID/5343cc

MAXIMUM POWER
228bhp/295bhp

CHASSIS/SUSPENSION
Unit-body monocoque body/chassis; coil spring and wishbone ifs; coil spring, wishbone and fixed-length drive shaft irs

BODY STYLE
2 seater Cabriolet, by Jaguar

TOP SPEED
141mph/227kph
(153mph/246kph for V12)

0-60MPH
7.4 seconds
(6.5 seconds for V12)

Although Jaguar's E-Type sports car had been a great success, the car which took over from it in 1975 was an entirely different sort of sporting car. Whereas the E-Type had been descended from a racing sports-car design, the new XJ-S was really a short-wheelbase, more sporting derivative of the current Jaguar saloons.

For the first eight years of its life, indeed, the XJ-S was only available as a close-coupled four-seater with fixed-head coupe styling and the powerful but 'gas-guzzling' V12 engine. It was not until the autumn of 1983 that Jaguar produced a cabriolet version of the XJ-S, and at the same time a brand-new twin-cam six-cylinder engine, the AJ6 unit, was also put on sale. This was mainly intended for the 'XJ40' saloon car, which appeared in 1986, and was improved in detail during its 'trial run' in the XJ-S model.

Because the XJ-S was based on XJ6 saloon-car engineering, it was a solidly proportioned car built around pressed-steel panels, with impressive ride and handling and very high performance. Although, as usual, this was a Jaguar shaped by the company's founder and chairman, Sir William Lyons, and was long, low, wide and carefully detailed, it was not quite as elegant as usual, owing to the use of stabilizing aerodynamic 'sail' panels at the rear quarters.

The V12 engine, though magnificent and powerful, was also very large, and even in 'HE' form (from 1981) it was quite thirsty, but it provided so much performance that the customers were always present. It was, without a doubt, one of the most silkily silent big engines in the world; it was almost impossible to tell that a V12-engined XJ-S's engine was running when it was merely turning over at idle speeds.

The cabriolet of 1983 used the same basic body lines as the coupe, except that the entire top and rear of the body were re-shaped. The sail panels, thankfully, disappeared completely, the accommodation was cut down to two seats (with stowage space behind), yet like other such 'conversions' (notably the Baur-bodied BMWs) the car retained fixed rails around the door glasses, as well as a strengthening brace across the car between the pillars, above and behind the passengers' heads. A 'Targa' panel in the roof itself was, of course, removable. The soft top itself was well-padded and tucked down into the area previously reserved for the rear seats of the coupe. Luggage accommodation was as generous as that in the coupe model.

At first this body style was produced by Aston Martin Tickford on Jaguar's behalf, with the new six-cylinder engine only. Within two years, however, final assembly had been moved 'in house' to Jaguar's own plant, and the more powerful V12 engine was made available.

Even though this was an attractive alternative to the closed XJ-S, it was still not a true convertible, and the customers continued to demand such a car. Clearly Jaguar management listened to them, for development of a full convertible was put in hand for launch towards the end of the

LEFT Below the waistline, and ahead of the screen, the open-top SC looks the same as the XJ-S Coupe. Only the roof and the controversial 'sail' panels have been discarded.

LEFT, BELOW With the soft-top furled, the XJ-SC was a genuine open-top car, but it still had a roll-cage for occupant protection, and rigid window surrounds.

BELOW Because of the rather bulky fold-back soft-top fitted to the XJ-SC, there was no space for rear seats. The XJ-S was a generous 2+2 model, whereas the XJ-SC was a two-seater.

BELOW Jaguar's XJ-S style was introduced in 1975, but the open-top version, called XJ-SC, did not appear until 1983. This is the 'rest of the World' type, for USA-market models have four circular headlamps.

JEEP WORLD WAR TWO TYPE

PRODUCTION SPAN
1941 to date

ENGINE
4-cyl, sv

CAPACITY
134 CID/2199cc

MAXIMUM POWER
60bhp

CHASSIS/SUSPENSION
Ladder-style chassis frame, half-elliptic leaf spring beam front, half-elliptic leaf spring rear

BODY STYLE
4 seater Roadster, by Willys

TOP SPEED
30mph/97kph approx

0-60MPH
25.0 seconds approx

In World War I, much of an army's mobility relied on the use of horses, but in World War II the troops had to be mechanized. To satisfy an army's demand for such transport, whole generations of new vehicles had to be developed.

Before it was drawn into the fighting, the United States Army set out to find a new and versatile type of vehicle, a lightweight device with 'go-anywhere' capability which could replace horses. Such a vehicle was to be a 'General Purpose' or 'GP' machine – and it was not long before this acronym was modified to read 'Jeep'.

The original design of such a vehicle was by Bantam, but massive production contracts for a much-developed machine went to Willys and Ford-USA, both of whom produced hundreds of thousands of vehicles. The Jeep used a rugged 2.2-litre/134 CID side-valve engine in a solid chassis, and got its go-anywhere reputation by being short and high off the ground, and by having four-wheel drive.

The body style is best described as 'functional', for it owed nothing to a styling department, and there were no luxury features of any type. The wheel arches were only there to keep water and mud out of the passenger compartment (but they often failed to do that!), the seats were small, hard and not intended to be other than serviceable, and the weather protection was only approximate.

Jeeps had high screens and sometimes used a canvas soft top stretched over a rudimentary frame, but side curtains did not figure, and most of them spent most of their time churning round as true open four-wheel-drive models. In theory, a Jeep could carry four, but was often loaded with more, and its occupants ranged from generals to privates. There was no luggage accommodation, the spare wheel was clamped to the exterior of the body and it was often said that the most useful Jeep was one which brought along a sister car, to increase the payload.

No matter. Until and unless its chassis ground to a halt on rough ground, a Jeep could be driven across almost every type of terrain, and even a high-ranking officer would prefer to trust a Jeep, rather than a limousine, to get him around the battlefield. Jeeps were not very fast, and had a very hard ride, especially if the roads used were uneven. They were not only extremely rugged, but also they were eventually in universal supply. It was often cheaper to indent for a new Jeep rather than to bother to repair a broken one, and tens of thousands were simply abandoned, close to a battlefield, where they had broken down.

Not only is the original Jeep remembered with affection by countless numbers of ex-servicemen (for its enormous charisma and cheeky character), but it was responsible for many subsequent four-wheel-drive machines. Civilian Jeeps are still produced to this day, the British Land-Rover started life as a straight copy of the Jeep, but with British running gear, and similar four-wheel-drive machines are now built in every motoring continent.

RIGHT Even though few Jeeps actually carried weapons, they were probably the most important Allied vehicles of the Second World War period. There isn't an inch of unnecessary decoration in the style.

OPPOSITE, INSET The Jeep could carry four passengers, or some stores, but not both. Soft-tops were rarely erected, unless the weather was terrible.

FOR OFFICIAL
USE ONLY
US ARMY
MAX 55
MPH
DKE 856C
WILLYS
MB 1943

LANCIA AURELIA SPIDER

PRODUCTION SPAN
1954–1958

ENGINE
V6, ohv

CAPACITY
147 CID/2451cc

MAXIMUM POWER
118bhp

CHASSIS/SUSPENSION
Unit-body monocoque structure, coil springsliding pillar ifs, half-elliptic leaf spring and De Dion rear

BODY STYLE
2 seater Roadster, by Pininfarina

TOP SPEED
108mph/174kph

0–60MPH
12.5 seconds

Of all the many sporting marques of Italy, Lancia has one of the longest and most distinguished histories. Many of its cars were technically advanced when announced, and for many years the company's 'vee' engines were quite unlike those of any of its rivals.

In the early 1950s the company excelled itself. Not only did Lancia announce the new medium-sized Aurelia family car, which had a front engine and a rear-mounted transmission (like the Porsche 924/944, but a quarter of a century before that car was launched), but it also gave rise to a pair of exquisitely shaped sporting derivatives. Within a year, the saloon had been joined by the beautiful Pininfarina-styled GT Coupe, which set the standard for many future fastbacks to follow. Three years after that, Pininfarina also collaborated on the design of an open version of the car – the Aurelia Spider – which had an even shorter wheelbase, and was specially intended for the North American market.

Both the running gear and the styling of the Spider were notable. The saloon naturally used a steel-panelled unit-construction shell, but it was still possible for its underframe to be used as the basis of shorter-wheelbase sporty models. The body shape, by one of Italy's most famous styling houses, was sexily curvaceous and attractive, and used a wrapped-round windscreen in the latest transatlantic fashion. The Spider retained the traditional Lancia front grille, and had all the flair of a custom-built Italian sports car. The original Spiders had detachable side curtains, and were dubbed 'America', though later types had a more conventional European-style windscreen shape, as well as wind-up door windows.

The running gear, like that of all current Aurelia models, not only featured a powerful V6 engine and had the rear-mounted transmission, but there was also the long-established Lancia sliding pillar front suspension and De Dion rear suspension. By any standards, and especially compared with some so-called modern sporting cars being produced in other countries, the Aurelia was an advanced and attractive package.

Not only that, but the Spider had a great deal of Italian character (some rival concerns were sure that Italian firms had engineers employed to do nothing else but put back the character lost by mass-production design!), was well-balanced and was a well-packaged sports car. It didn't seem to matter that it was quite expensive, for Lancias were never made in sufficient quantities to get the price down any further.

ABOVE The Aurelia Spider's instrument display was typical of Italian cars of the 1950s. Most prominent, naturally, is the speedometer.

OPPOSITE The Aurelia Spider's original style was by Pininfarina, who included several 'Detroit' touches to the shape, including the wrap-round windscreen, later types were fitted with a more conventional screen shape, allied to wind-up door glasses.

BELOW RIGHT Lancia's shield badge fits proudly to the famous grille, the result being an aggressive, but pleasing, sports car body style.

14 GXB

LINCOLN CONTINENTAL MK 1

PRODUCTION SPAN
1940–1948

ENGINE
V12, sv

CAPACITY
290 CID/4784cc

MAXIMUM POWER
120bhp

CHASSIS/SUSPENSION
Ladder-style chassis frame, transverse leaf spring front beam, transverse leaf spring rear

BODY STYLE
5 seater Convertible (or Saloon), by Ford-USA

TOP SPEED
85mph/137kph approx

0-60MPH
Not known

Lincoln, once a proudly independent concern, had been bought up by Ford in the 1920s, though it continued to use unique running gear for some years to come. By the late 1930s the marque had been devalued, so that a 'Lincoln' was really only an up-market Ford. Henry Ford's son Edsel, who was already president of the Ford Motor Co., decided to make Lincoln a distinctive car once again, and the original Continental of 1940 was the result.

This was the first Lincoln, for many years, in which styling and equipment took precedence over cost control. Lincoln devotees like to ignore the fact that under its elegant skin the Continental was no more than a mildly reworked Lincoln Zephyr, with the same 125in/317cm wheelbase chassis, and 75 degree side-valve V12 engine.

Suspension, as on other Fords, Mercurys and Lincolns of the period, featured transverse leaf springs and beam axles at front and rear. This was due to Henry Ford's personal edict; Edsel would have liked to emulate the competition from General Motors, which had independent front suspension. For the special Continental application, the engine was given aluminium cylinder heads, while the three-speed gearbox was joined by a two-speed Columbia rear axle. In 1942 there was a short-lived 5-litre/306 CID engine, and an unpopular 'Liquimatic' automatic transmission; a more successful overdrive option replaced the two-speed axle.

The original Continental Mk 1 (later to become known, simply, as the 'Mark') was announced in 1940, and was available either as a two-door fixed-head coupe, or a two-door convertible. At first, one of the most obvious recognition points was the use of an exposed spare wheel, but in later months this was given a cover.

At the front, the original 'Mark' looked much like every other Lincoln-Zephyr, with its headlamps recessed in the wings and with a two-part grille divided by a sharp prow over the radiator. For 1942 (which was a very short selling season, prior to entry into the Second World War), the front end was restyled, with squarer front wings.

It was in its profile – long, smooth and carefully detailed – and in its detail finish that the Mark was such an advance over any other Ford or Lincoln-Mercury product. There were no running boards, the Cabriolet soft top was superbly tailored and there was little evidence of Detroit 'jazz' in the detailing. Edsel Ford, who died in 1943, always intended that the Mark should be equal to, if not better than, the Cadillac, and in terms of style and equipment this aim certainly succeeded. This explains the fitments of the Lincoln-Zephyr Town Limousine's instrument panel, and gold-accented finish of interior trim and hardware. The cylinder heads were of polished aluminium, as were the manifolds, and even the cylinder head nuts were chrome-plated. Vacuum window lifts were fitted.

Even though the Mark sold better after the war than before it, it was dropped in 1948 when the high cost of hand-crafting the interior could no longer be justified.

RIGHT Like other Lincolns of the period, the Continental Mark 1 had a distinctive nose, featuring grilles at each side of the commanding prow.

BELOW The original Lincoln Continental, launched in 1940, was masterminded by Henry Ford's son Edsel. Although it shared its chassis and running gear with the current Lincoln Zephyr, it had a unique body style, so elegant for the period that it became an instant 'classic'.

MASERATI 3500GT, SEBRING AND MISTRAL SPIDER

PRODUCTION SPAN
1957–1970

ENGINE
6-cyl, 2 ohc

CAPACITY
213 CID/3485cc;
225 CID/3695cc;
245 CID/4014cc

MAXIMUM POWER
220 to 255bhp, depending on engine and application

CHASSIS/SUSPENSION
Separate chassis frame, coil spring and wishbone ifs, half-elliptic leaf spring and radius arm rear

BODY STYLE
2 seater Convertibles, by Touring, Vignale, Frua

TOP SPEED
140mph/225kph to 150mph/241kph, depending on body style and engine

0-60MPH
8.0 seconds approx

Before the 1950s, Maserati of Italy was known as a racing-car constructor that built a few road cars. After the first of the six-cylinder cars, the 3500GT, was put on sale, the situation was quickly reversed.

Maserati, like all its rivals in the Italian 'Supercar' business at the time, was quick to design and develop new engines, chassis and mechanical parts, but was not large enough to make bodies. Every car in the long-running six-cylinder-engined series, therefore, had bodies whose style was approved by Maserati, but which were built by independent coachbuilders.

The 3500GT which founded this family had a simple chassis, with tubular side members and a great deal of sheet steel reinforcement. The chassis cradled a powerful and reliable twin-overhead-camshaft six-cylinder unit which had evolved from the engines used in Maserati racing cars of the early and mid-1950s. The same chassis, in one of several different wheelbase lengths, was used for 13 years.

Early cars were 220bhp 3500GTs, and had engines with carburettors and drum brakes, but discs were offered from 1959, a five-speed gearbox soon followed, and fuel injection was adopted in 1961. Except that the engine was twice enlarged in the next few years, the design then stabilized throughout the 1960s.

In most cases there was a choice between 2+2 coupe, and open two-seater convertible styling, although the interim Sebring model was only ever sold as a Coupe. For the 3500GT/3500GTI range, Vignale of Turin built almost all 'Spider' bodies, while Frua was responsible for open *and* closed styles on the later Mistral model.

The Vignale Spider was lovely, as you might expect from a late-1950s Italian creation, with a flowing profile, and a forward-thrusting rectangular grille which was so characteristic of this model. The famous Maserati 'trident' trade mark was properly in evidence, as was a slim air scoop in the bonnet top. Vignale also offered a detachable hardtop for this body which, when fitted, made it look almost the same as the Touring-bodied fixed-head coupe.

The Mistral, by Frua, was an altogether more sensuous, and curvaceous, style, with a low and wide snout, a larger and more curved screen, and an optional hardtop which did nothing for the overall effect. Its style, ahead of the screen and in general proportions, was the same as that of the Coupe, which was also built by Frua.

Inside these first-generation Maserati road cars there was usually an aluminium-spoked wood-rim wheel, a full display of instruments and a rather haphazard layout of switches and controls. All the cars, naturally, were very fast. It is a quirk of history that they are not now remembered with as much affection as are the Ferraris of the day, even though they outsold their deadly rival at the time.

LEFT Several Italian coachbuilders produced bodies for Maserati's six-cylinder engined chassis of the 1957-1970 period. The Mistral, built either as a fast-back coupe, or as a Spider, was by Frua. The same company also produced shells for AC and Monteverdi at the time, the similarities being obvious.

BELOW The Frua-styled Mistral was elegant without being ostentatious, and comfortable without being too large. Suitably engined, a Mistral could reach 150mph/241kph.

MERCEDES-BENZ 500K & 540K

CABRIOLET

PRODUCTION SPAN
1934–1939

ENGINE
8-cyl, ohv

CAPACITY
306 CID/5018cc;
330 CID/5401cc

MAXIMUM POWER
160/180bhp

CHASSIS/SUSPENSION
Separate chassis frame, coil spring and wishbone ifs, coil spring/swing axle irs

BODY STYLE
2 seater and 4 seater Cabriolets, by Daimler-Benz

TOP SPEED
100mph/161kph to 105mph/169kph, depending on body style

0-60MPH
16.5/15.0 seconds approx

Daimler (who built Mercedes cars) had got together with Benz in 1926, thus founding the Mercedes-Benz marque, a company which was to grow steadily in the next two generations. Not even the awful carnage of war could destroy the marque's heritage completely, so Mercedes-Benz is as dominant today as it was 60 years ago.

There had been supercharged, ultra-sporting, eight-cylinder Mercedes-Benz cars in the 1920s, but a new generation of 'blown eights', designed by Hans Nibel's team and launched in 1933, were much less sporting, but much more versatile than before. The original 'Nibel eight' was the short-lived 380K of 1933-1934, but the cars which are more easily remembered are the 500K of 1934-1936, and the larger-engined 540K of 1936-1939.

Each of these cars was based on a massive, but softly sprung, chassis with all independent suspension. The swing-axle rear layout could give rise to sudden oversteer accompanied by a loss of tyre grip.

As with the 1920s-style range, all these cars had straight-eight-cylinder engines, with 'optional' supercharging. In normal motoring the supercharger was not actually working, but if the throttle was then fully depressed it clutched in the 'blower', there was a characteristic scream from this component, a lot more power was suddenly developed and fuel consumption rose alarmingly. In effect, this meant that the cars had a choice of engines, and explains why, for instance, a 540K was rated at 115 *or* 180bhp.

Mercedes-Benz stylists were in their element when producing a whole range of flamboyant body shapes for these cars. This was a period when the German motor industry was at its most expansive, when Daimler-Benz could sell every car it built and when the cars' looks reflected this confidence. Some cars were closed coupes, but most were Cabriolets, and all had the same vee-section radiator grille topped off by the three-pointed star which is still found on current-model Mercedes-Benz cars.

Styles tended to be fully blown, with curving front and rear wings, and with free-standing headlamps, but the 1920s-style chrome-plated and exposed exhaust pipes were also retained, these protruding through the bonnet panel on the right side. Two-tone coachwork was normal, many cars had wire-spoked wheels and the effect was rather more transatlantic than European.

The whole character of these cars reflected the political climate of Nazi Germany, for they looked, behaved and performed in a bombastic and self-assertive manner. Magazine testers used such phrases as 'insolent power' to describe their behaviour, and there is no doubt that few felt able or willing to argue with a 5,400lb/2,448kg K-Wagen in full flight.

The most amazing derivative of all – the 580K of 1939 – was killed off by the outbreak of war. What a car this might have been, for with the supercharger working it produced more than 200bhp, matched by a five-speed gearbox.

RIGHT The eight-cylinder engined 500K was built from 1934 to 1936, with a variety of extravagant but obviously Teutonic body styles.

BELOW RIGHT The larger-engined 540K took over from the 500K in 1936, though the chassis design was not altered. Body styles – particularly Cabriolet by Mercedes-Benz itself and produced at the Sindelfingen factory – were impressive, but there was only four-seater accommodation inside that massive shell.

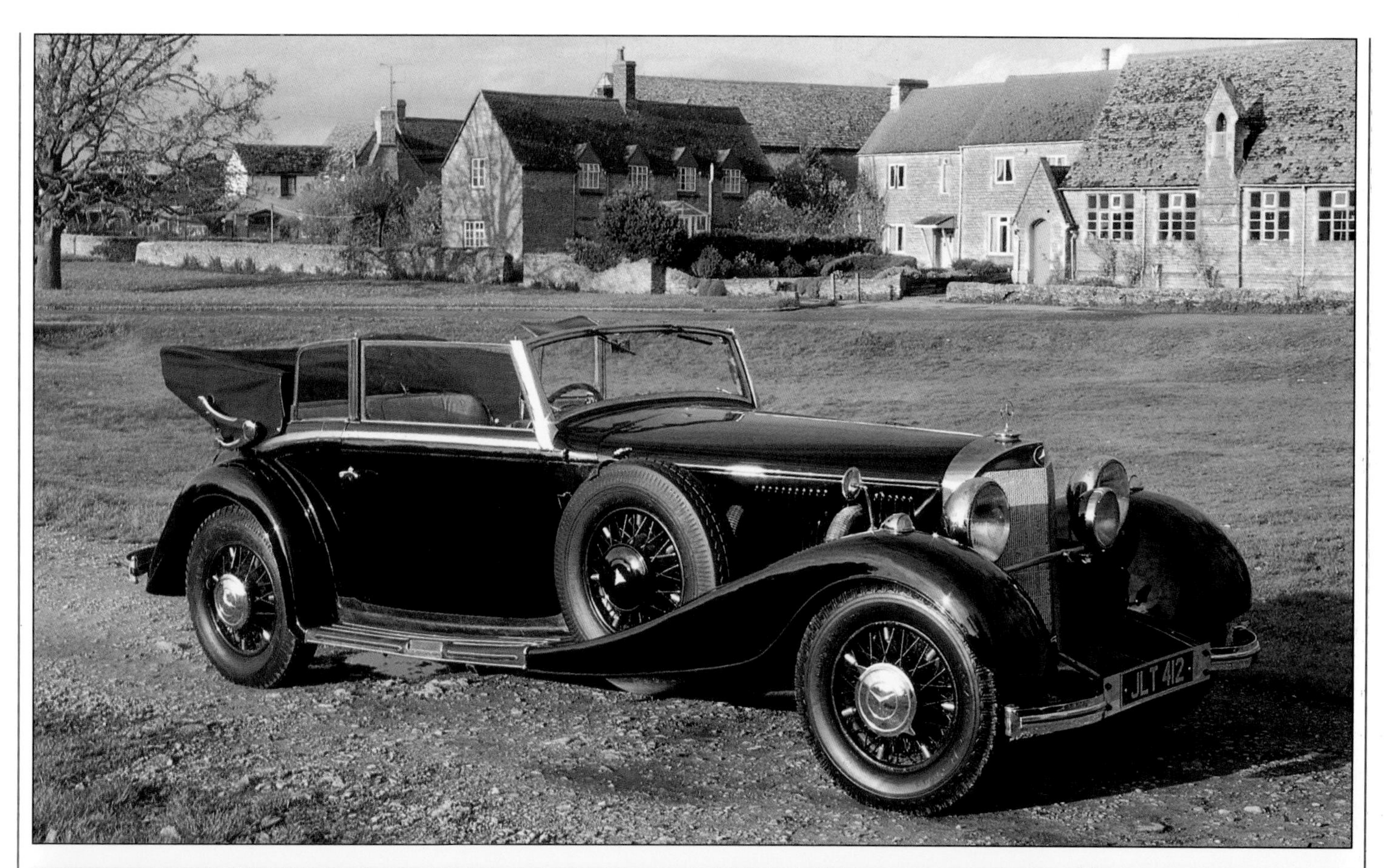
JLT 412

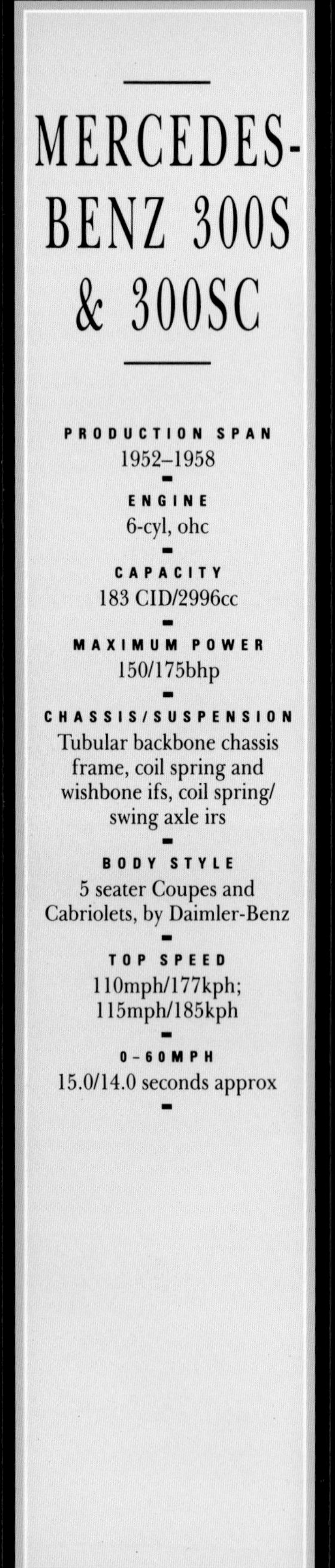

MERCEDES-BENZ 300S & 300SC

PRODUCTION SPAN
1952–1958

ENGINE
6-cyl, ohc

CAPACITY
183 CID/2996cc

MAXIMUM POWER
150/175bhp

CHASSIS/SUSPENSION
Tubular backbone chassis frame, coil spring and wishbone ifs, coil spring/ swing axle irs

BODY STYLE
5 seater Coupes and Cabriolets, by Daimler-Benz

TOP SPEED
110mph/177kph; 115mph/185kph

0-60MPH
15.0/14.0 seconds approx

During the Second World War, the Daimler-Benz factories had been flattened by bombing. It took years to get the business onto its feet again before a new, large, luxury Mercedes-Benz model could be introduced. The first derivative to be shown was the six-seater 300 saloon of 1951, and this was soon followed by the 300S Coupe and Cabriolet models.

In a gesture of defiance which paid off so handsomely in the years which followed, Fritz Nallinger's engineering team produced a car new from end to end – chassis, suspension, engine, transmission and body styles. Not only was the 300 range built in various styles, but much of the running gear was later used in the 300SL 'gull-wing' coupe which followed in 1954, though the 300SL had a space-frame chassis.

The backbone (literally) of all the 300 family was a tubular chassis frame, with all-independent suspension, and a six-cylinder overhead-cam engine of 2996cc/183 CID. The 300S had a 150bhp engine with carburettors, while the 300SC of 1955-1958 had 175bhp and Bosch fuel injection. At the rear of the chassis, there was an ingenious ride-selection arrangement, whereby the driver controlled the operation of electric motors which engaged and tightened a pair of auxiliary torsion bars.

Body shapes, whether of the large four-door six-seater 300 saloon, or of the more specialized Coupes and Cabriolets, were rounded and smooth, but something of a half-way house between 1930s and true post-war body styling; naturally the traditional Mercedes-Benz grille and three-pointed star were proudly displayed. The saloon rode on a 120in/305cm wheelbase, but Coupes and Cabriolets had a shorter 114.2in/290cm wheelbase instead.

While it was in production, the 300S/300SC type was Germany's most expensive car, and was bought by many rich celebrities. In every way, it was meant to be a successor to, and certainly a descendant of, the pre-war 540K types – progress was such that the 300S went significantly faster than a 540K had ever done, but with a much smaller engine.

There were three different body types, all sharing the same chassis and the same basic shape – these were described in catalogues as Roadster, Cabriolet and Coupe. Each had four seats, though the rear compartment was surprisingly restricted, and the luggage compartment was enormous.

The Roadster had a fully disappearing soft top, whereas the Cabriolet had the traditional type of German soft top complete with chromed landau irons; the Coupe was effectively a Roadster, minus soft top, but with a permanently fixed steel top. There was even more complication – an identically styled detachable hardtop was also available for Roadster types! All types had wind-up door windows, and the most sumptuous fittings.

Sales were very limited – with only 560 300S cars and 200 300SCs being built – so the model was allowed to die off gently in 1958.

RIGHT After the Second World War, the first post-war design from Mercedes-Benz was the six-cylinder engined 300 Series. The saloon was launched in 1951, but a year later it was joined by the splendidly equipped 300S Cabriolet.

RIGHT, BELOW From this, as from every other angle, there was no mistaking the Mercedes-Benz identity of the new 300S. In styling terms, this was a transitional model, with some 1950s features grafted on to late-1930s proportions.

OLC 3

MERCEDES-BENZ 230SL, 250SL & 280SL

PRODUCTION SPAN
1963–1971

ENGINE
6-cyl, ohc

CAPACITY
141 CID/2308cc;
152 CID/2496cc;
169 CID/2778cc

MAXIMUM POWER
150/170bhp

CHASSIS/SUSPENSION
Unit-body steel monocoque structure, coil spring and wishbone ifs, coil spring/ swing axle irs

BODY STYLE
2 seater Coupes and Roadsters, by Daimler-Benz

TOP SPEED
115mph/185kph to 120mph/193kph, depending on engine

0-60MPH
10.7/9.9 seconds, depending on engine

During the 1950s, Mercedes-Benz built a pair of sporting cars – the remarkable space-frame chassis 300SL ('gull-wing' and roadster), and the more mundane 190SL. In the early 1960s, however, it was decided that the two cars should be replaced by one new model, and Project W113 (or 230SL, when announced) was the result.

The new car, like other sporting models from Stuttgart, had a unique style, but was otherwise closely based on the engineering of other Mercedes-Benz family cars. In this case the 'donor' vehicle was really the 220SE saloon.

The new style, first seen in 1963, was not changed for eight years, though in that time three different engines – 2.3-litre, 2.5-litre and 2.8-litre (141, 152 and 170 CID) – were employed. Thus, the 230SL was produced from 1963 to 1966, the 250SL only in 1967 and the final 280SL after that. Those who have experienced all three types usually state that the early cars were the most sporting, while the latest were the most flexible, and the most civilized.

It was for its body styling, especially with the detachable coupe roof in place, that the W113 will always be remembered. The roof has what became known as the 'pagoda' feature, this being done not to reduce the height of the roofline, but to raise the sides so as to provide as much glass and all-round visibility as possible. In all other ways, however, the W113 was 'corporate-Mercedes-Benz' in its style, with vertical headlamp, turn-indicator clusters, a wide-mouth grille and a large three-pointed star as its central grille motif.

The interior of all these cars was well-upholstered and neatly trimmed, with a large stowage area behind the seats, too small for passengers, but often used to house animals or willing children. Fitted suitcases, for this area, were a useful option.

As with the earlier 300S range, and with more recent sporting cars from Stuttgart, the car could be supplied as a Roadster with fold-away hood, a pure Coupe with soft top not provided or as a combination of the two. The detachable top was a very substantial item, and needed two strong people to lift it into place, or to remove it.

Even though swing axle rear suspension was retained, the first 230SLs handled well (far better than the definitive 300SL of the 1950s had ever done), and felt like real sports cars. It was also a very strong car; 'works' prepared cars won important rough-road rallies in Europe.

Over the years, though, the 'image' of the current SL sports car changed progressively, yet subtly. Later models were certainly 'softer', with a more supple ride, and with manners more suited to swishing elegantly around town, rather than scrabbling up and down mountain passes. Not for nothing has the 280SL developed an image as a glossy and well-equipped machine. In 1971 it was replaced by the V8-engined 350SL, which was even more 'touring', and even less of a sports car, than the 280SL had ever been.

RIGHT The 230SL was launched in 1963, and was built in this basic form until 1971. Some cars were soft-top derivatives, but many were sold with the optional, removable, hardtop.

FAR RIGHT The 230SL, like the 250SL and 280SL models which followed, had vertical headlamp styles, and a wide-mouth grille, allied to the characteristic 'Pagoda' roof.

CENTRE RIGHT The driver of a 230SL had no excuse for not knowing how fast he was going. This was what met his eyes when he glanced through the steering wheel.

BOTTOM RIGHT The 350SL replaced the 280SL in 1971. It had a completely new structure and V8 engine.

195 DP

195 DP

60
80
40
100
20
120
0
140
MPH
VDO
TANK
30
40
20
50
10
60
70
VDO

R EK 310

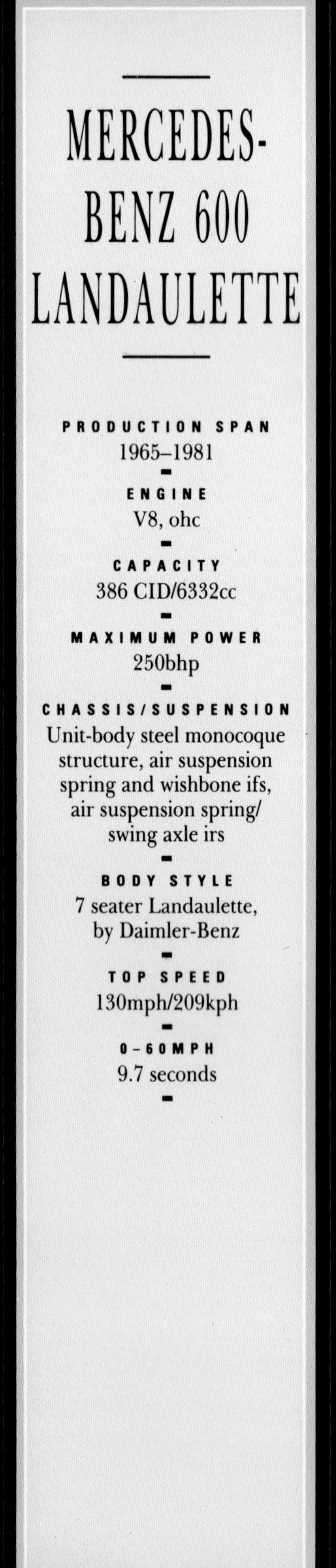

MERCEDES-BENZ 600 LANDAULETTE

PRODUCTION SPAN
1965–1981

ENGINE
V8, ohc

CAPACITY
386 CID/6332cc

MAXIMUM POWER
250bhp

CHASSIS/SUSPENSION
Unit-body steel monocoque structure, air suspension spring and wishbone ifs, air suspension spring/ swing axle irs

BODY STYLE
7 seater Landaulette, by Daimler-Benz

TOP SPEED
130mph/209kph

0–60MPH
9.7 seconds

The most famous pre-war Mercedes-Benz car had been the massive *Grosser* model, and by the 1960s the time seemed ripe for a new version of such a car to be built. The huge Type 600, which remained in production for nearly 20 years, was an excellent way to fill such a need. It stands alone as the largest-ever Mercedes-Benz car to be sold in the post-war period, and it seems unlikely ever to be displaced from that pinnacle – a fully specified example could weigh more than 6,000lb/2,721kg.

The Type 600 *Grosser*, more prosaically known as W100 when it was being designed, was completely new. It had a unit-construction body shell, with a choice of long (126in/320cm) or gargantuan (153.5in/390cm) wheelbases, three or sometimes four windows per side and up to seven seats. Power came from a 250bhp V8 engine, the first-ever production V8 from Mercedes-Benz, and, naturally, automatic transmission was standard. There was hydraulic power-assistance for almost everything, the suspension was self-levelling, there were disc brakes all round, and when introduced the Type 600 was certainly built as carefully, and was much more complex, than the latest Rolls-Royce.

For the first two years, every 600 built had closed coachwork, but in 1965 a state Landaulette was also put on offer on the shorter of the two wheelbases. The four standard doors and the rear quarter windows were retained, as was a metal roof over the front-seat occupants, while there was a bulky fold-down soft top at the rear which could cover all the rear-compartment passengers, or give them draught-free and very elegant open-top motoring. Both types had identical styling, with long straight-through lines in profile and rounded corners, but otherwise very square and upright looks. There was a great deal of brightwork to give a lighter touch to what would otherwise have been a rather ponderous machine.

The charm of the extremely expensive 600 model was not only that it had a superb soft ride, impressive stability and a top speed of around 130mph/209kph, but it was also a machine which could be, and usually was, driven very slowly indeed, on ceremonial occasions. Trim and furnishings – acres of wood, leather and related fittings – were all the highest possible standard and there was a great deal of passenger accommodation in the rear seat. Although it was a complex machine, the 600 was also known to be impressively reliable if maintained according to the thorough Daimler-Benz concern's recommendations. Almost every Type 600 was chauffeur-driven, and many were bought by business tycoons, royalty or heads of state. To buy a 600, it seemed, was politically more advisable for many personalities who did not want to be seen aligning themselves with the USA (a Cadillac) or the UK (a Rolls-Royce).

Because of the inordinate prices charged, the 600 was rare enough, and the Landaulette was even rarer than that. In 18 years, just 2,677 Type 600s were produced, of which a mere 59 had Landaulette coachwork.

RIGHT Room enough, surely, for any potentate and his entourage – this Mercedes-Benz 600 Landaulette has six passenger doors, and three rows of seats.

CENTRE Mercedes-Benz 600s were so luxuriously equipped that even the rearward facing 'jump seats' look inviting.

BOTTOM In extra-long-wheelbase form, the Mercedes-Benz 600 was an imposing, almost improbable, sight. This Landaulette has a mere seven seats, but is so large that it really needs two parking spaces to accommodate it.

MG TC

PRODUCTION SPAN
1945–1949

ENGINE
4-cyl, ohv

CAPACITY
76 CID/1250cc

MAXIMUM POWER
54bhp

CHASSIS/SUSPENSION
Ladder-style chassis frame, half-elliptic leaf spring front beam, half-elliptic leaf spring rear

BODY STYLE
2 seater Roadster, by MG

TOP SPEED
75mph/121kph

0-60MPH
22.7 seconds

MG's reputation for building simple and effective sports cars was built, in Oxford, in the 1920s, but it was with the launch of the first Midget, in 1928, that the appeal became universal. For the next 27 years there was always a Midget in the range, and this was always MG's best-selling model.

The T-Series dynasty was founded in 1936, following a corporate revolution at Nuffield. The TA was the first sports car designed at Morris Motors, rather than by MG itself. Except that a simpler overhead valve engine was used, the basic design layout of the car was unchanged – the TA, like the P-Series cars it replaced, had a simple chassis frame, front and rear suspension by beam axles and half-elliptic springs, and traditional body styling with sweeping front wings and free-standing headlamps.

The TA gave way to the TB in 1939, when a more modern engine was specified, but the outbreak of war soon put a stop to all MG sports-car sales. In 1945, when car assembly was resumed, the TB was lightly revised and put on sale again as the TC.

Although by that time it was beginning to look a touch old-fashioned, the TC was a great success, and introduced the MG marque to the important United States market. The TC was always a right-hand-drive car, but as it was so slim and manoeuvrable the Americans loved it anyway!

The TC was a rugged and simple little car, easy to build and equally easy to maintain. The body shell was built up around a wooden skeleton, with steel panels, and in most cases the car was used fully open. In this state, it was possible to fold the screen flat; some customers installed aero screens to give themselves a modicum of shelter.

When the weather was so bad that even a sports-car enthusiast had to hide himself away, there was a simple fold-away soft top which clipped to the screen rail and skimpy plastic side curtains which plugged into the cutaway doors and to the rear quarters behind the doors. Thus fitted out, the TC was waterproof, but by no means wind-proof, and since a heater was not usually fitted it meant that cold-climate owners had to be prepared to dress up for long journeys. Luggage, if any, was normally stowed behind the bench seat, but it was also possible to buy a luggage rack to drape over the exposed spare wheel.

The joys of MG Midget motoring were not in the straight-line performance of the car, but in the sheer joyful way that the car could be urged along twisty roads. It did not seem to matter that the suspension was very hard, nor that the tyres were narrow, for the car could almost be willed, rather than driven, round every corner.

It would not be an exaggeration to suggest that the MG TC was the car which paved the way for every other British sports car to sell so well in world markets, and it is still the model thought to be so typical of the MG marque. Yet only 10,000 TCs were built – perhaps every one of them was remembered with affection?

RIGHT The MG TC of 1945-1950 was the final flowering of a body style introduced in the early 1930s. Recognition points included the proud vertical radiator grille, the free-standing headlamps, the flowing wing line, and the exposed fuel tank and spare wheel.

BELOW RIGHT The MG TC was nothing if not practical. Side curtains could be plugged in to the doors to protect the driver in wet weather, but many owners never troubled to do this. The soft-top was a simple fold-away device which lived behind the seats when furled.

MG MIDGET

PRODUCTION SPAN
1961–1979

ENGINE
4-cyl, ohv

CAPACITY
58 CID/948cc;
67 CID/1098cc;
78 CID/1275cc;
91 CID/1493cc

MAXIMUM POWER
46/56/59/65/66bhp

CHASSIS/SUSPENSION
Unit-body monocoque structure, coil spring and wishbone ifs, quarter-elliptic (later half-elliptic) leaf spring rear

BODY STYLE
2 seater Roadster, by BMC

TOP SPEED
86mph/138kph to 101mph/163kph, depending on engine

0-60MPH
20.5 to 12.3 seconds, depending on engine

After the MG TF Midget was replaced by the smooth new MGA in 1955, BMC put the model name 'Midget' back into its trademarks drawer. It would be another six years before it reappeared.

In the meantime, a new small-engined Austin-Healey sports car, the Sprite, was launched in 1958, and when the time came for it to be restyled in 1961, it was relaunched as *two* cars, the Austin-Healey Sprite Mk II and a sister car called the MG Midget Mk I. For the next decade two differently badged sports cars were marketed on the same basis, but from 1971 the Sprite name was discontinued and the MG Midget carried on, on its own, until 1979.

The basic engineering of the Midget, therefore, was of a Healey family design, which used modified running gear from BMC's two small cars, the Austin A35 and the Morris Minor saloons. It had a sturdily engineered monocoque body/chassis unit with, in its original guise, a rear axle slung on cantilever leaf springs and radius arms.

The Sprite of 1958 had featured 'frog eye' headlamp mountings, and no external access to the boot, but the 1961 restyle produced a more conventional-looking machine with a rather plain front end, and a lockable boot lid in the tail. Legend has it that the Healeys were responsible for the nose, and MG's own designers for the tail! One of the most popular options was a removable hardtop. The 1961-1964 version of the Midget was equipped with detachable side screens, and a build-it-yourself soft top and folding frame. The car was small, and had a somewhat tight-fitting cockpit and rather basic trim and instrumentation.

Over the years, and in acute competition with the rival Triumph Spitfire, the Midget was gradually but persistently improved. In its 18-year career, the Midget was never significantly restyled, though from mid-1964 the shell was given a larger windscreen and wind-up door windows, a foldaway soft top followed later, and for 1975 it was necessary to add large and deformable black bumpers, front and rear, to meet burgeoning USA legislation.

To keep up with its competition, the Midget was regularly given more powerful and free-revving engines. There was a 1.1-litre/67 CID engine for 1963, a more powerful version of the same in 1964 and a very tuneable 1.3-litre/78 CID enlargement of it for 1967. Then, for 1975, came the ultimate insult, as far as MG fans were concerned – the Midget inherited the 1,493cc/91 CID engine of the Triumph Spitfire! The last Midget, in fact, was the only derivative which could reach a genuine 100mph/161kph (at least in European-standard tune), and was still a nippy, characterful and somehow enthusiastic little sports car which made a multitude of friends.

Nevertheless, by the end of the 1970s the Midget was well overdue for replacement, especially as the mid-engined Fiat X1/9 had made all traditional sports-car designs look obsolete. But British Leyland had no plans for a new model, and the old-style Midget died off gracefully in 1979.

ABOVE MG Midget shapes changed very little indeed over the years. By the early 1970s, as shown here, the car had grown wind-up door windows, and for a short period it was also built with circular style instead of flat-top rear wheel arch cutouts.

OPPOSITE, TOP LEFT Folding up the soft-top of an early 1970s MG Midget – a quicker and altogether more practical process than with the original 'build-it-yourself' variety.

OPPOSITE, TOP RIGHT MG Midgets were small two-seater sports cars with a high 'fun coefficient'. The roll-over bar fitted to this car is an after-market accessory.

BELOW RIGHT The MG Midget was also built in 'badge engineered' form as an Austin-Healey Sprite. The only visual difference was to the badging and decoration of the car – this was an MG, as the familiar octagonal-shaped badge shows.

RNK 776M
MIDGET

MORGAN PLUS 8

PRODUCTION SPAN
1968 to date

ENGINE
V8, ohv

CAPACITY
215 CID/3528cc

MAXIMUM POWER
151/153/155/190bhp

CHASSIS/SUSPENSION
Ladder-style chassis frame, coil spring and sliding pillar ifs, half-elliptic leaf spring rear

BODY STYLE
2 seater Roadster, by Morgan

TOP SPEED
125mph/201kph

0-60MPH
6.5/5.6 seconds, depending on engine tune

Morgan introduced its first four-wheeler in 1935, and its styling has remained in a time-warp ever since. The type of construction has not been altered, and except for certain smoothing-out operations at the front and the rear the shape of the car is very much as before. It is often said that a new Morgan is as close to a 50-year-old 'classic' as can be found anywhere in the world.

Earlier Morgans had four-cylinder engines, latterly Triumph TR units bought from Standard-Triumph, but when the supply ran out a new engine was necessary. It was at this point that the company turned to Rover, arranged to take supplies of the light-alloy 3.5-litre/215 CID V8 unit, and the Morgan Plus 8 was born. By the late 1980s it had been on sale for nearly 20 years, without any sign of a redesign, and without any sign of flagging demand.

The Plus 8, like every other Morgan, took shape at Malvern Link around the basis of a simple, ladder-style chassis frame. This used the sliding pillar type of independent front suspension with which every Morgan had been fitted since the first tricycle had taken to the road in 1910.

Like every other Morgan, too, the Plus 8 had a very hard ride, but it was undeniably a hairy-chested sports car. Because of the huge torque available, it had astonishing acceleration, and the rush to the horizon was only eventually slowed by the old-fashioned aerodynamics.

The body shell had a wooden skeleton, to which the steel or aluminium skin panels were fixed. The stance was so low that, helped by the cutaway doors, it was possible for the passenger to put his arm out of the side of the body shell and touch the ground without straining his posture.

There was a fixed windscreen, and a simple fold-away soft top which was stowed in a pouch behind the passenger compartment. Like every other traditional Morgan, the Plus 8 had removable sidescreens, with sliding perspex panels, and a fold-out flap through which the driver could make hand signals. The seats were well-padded, but placed low, and the passengers' legs were near-horizontal, at each side of a prominent transmission tunnel.

Except for a small area behind the seats, there was no enclosed stowage compartment; most Plus 8 owners strapped their cases to a luggage rack on the tail.

Development, and change, came slowly at Morgan; but in the first 20 years the engine was gradually made more powerful, the entire gearbox was changed on two occasions, a rack-and-pinion steering installation became available and the whole car became wider to match the latest tyres and wheels.

Morgans either attract hate or adulation, but the company never found any problems in maintaining a healthy waiting list for these extrovert machines. A typical Plus 8 customer waited in line for years, got used to the bone-shattering ride and usually fell in love with the performance and the exuberant character. Then, as likely as not, he went out and ordered another one!

RIGHT Born in the 1930s, refined over the last half-century, the Morgan sports style changed only gradually from year to year. This rakish Plus 8 was actually built in 1982-1983.

FAR RIGHT The Morgan Plus Eight facia and instrument layout was logical, complete, and easy to read. Note the traditional type of cutaway doors, with pockets for map stowage.

LOWER RIGHT Except that wheels have become fatter, the front end style of the Plus Eight, complete with podded headlamps and a traditional type of chrome bumper, is just the same as it was in the mid-1950s.

BLU 94Y

MORRIS MINOR

PRODUCTION SPAN
1948–1971

ENGINE
4-cyl, sv and ohv

CAPACITY
49 CID/803cc;
56 CID/918cc;
58 CID/948cc;
68 CID/1098cc

MAXIMUM POWER
27/30/37/48bhp

CHASSIS/SUSPENSION
Unit-body monocoque structure, torsion bar and wishbone ifs, half-elliptic leaf spring rear

BODY STYLE
4 seater Convertible, by BMC

TOP SPEED
60mph/97kph to 75mph/121kph, depending on engine

0-60MPH
50 seconds approx to 24 seconds, depending on engine

During the Second World War, Britain's motor industry was turned over completely to producing military machinery of all types, but a few designers still found time to plan ahead for the new models they wanted to put on sale afterwards. It was in this way that Alec Issigonis of Morris Motors, encouraged by the company's vice-chairman, Sir Miles Thomas, got work under way on the Morris Minor.

Compared with all previous small Morris cars, the new Minor (which was once going to be called 'Mosquito') was technically advanced. Except that it originally used an old side-valve engine (from the 1930s-style Morris Eight model), it was a completely new design. With its rounded and altogether unmistakable looks, it was launched in October 1948 and remained on sale, in a whole variety of guises, for the next 23 years. Although it had been an expensive car to design, develop and prepare for manufacture, its long production run (during which more than 1.5 million examples were produced) paid ample dividends.

The secret of the new design was the use of a very rigid unitary steel body/chassis unit, which had much of its strength in the underside. This, with many modifications, not only allowed saloon, estate car, van and pick-up types to be sold, but there was also a very popular convertible, known throughout its life as the Tourer.

Behind the windscreen, and below the waistline, this car was effectively a chop-top two-door saloon, and retained the same four-seater passenger accommodation. The very first Tourers were completely open-topped behind the doors, but shortly a revised style was phased in, with permanent rear quarter windows and a rail for the soft top to seal up against. The soft top itself folded back to the front edge of the boot lid, and could be covered by a pouch, but as this was a budget-priced family model there was no question of giving the soft top a container in which to hide.

All Minors were fitted with supple torsion bar independent front suspension. This, allied to precise rack-and-pinion steering, gave the Minor the agile roadholding for which it is remembered to this day. It was always a chassis which could have used significantly more engine power, and production cars always felt reassuringly under-powered. At first, the Minor had its headlamps mounted low down, at each side of the radiator grille, but from the early 1950s the definitive position, with each headlamp mounted in a pod at the front of the wing, was standardized.

The old side-valve engine gave way to a new overhead-valve BMC unit in the early 1950s and this, in more and yet more powerful guise, was retained until the end of production in 1971; a 1.1-litre/67 CID unit was fitted from late 1962. The vee-screen gave way to a curved one-piece screen in 1956, at which point the enlarged engine gave it the 'Minor 1000' title, but after the end of the 1950s little further development took place, and the car gradually died away. Even so, something of a Morris Minor 'cult' grew up as interest in classic cars developed in the 1970s.

INSET The Morris Minor Convertible is one of the most easily recognized car shapes of all. Original cars had low mounted headlamps, but from the early 1950s all derivatives had headlamps mounted high up in the front wings.

OPPOSITE Alec Issigonis's Morris Minor was launched in 1948 and built, with several different sizes of engine, until 1971; there was always a convertible in the range. All had a great deal of character, but of course, not much performance.

142 DLR

PANTHER DE VILLE CABRIOLET

PRODUCTION SPAN
1974–1982

ENGINE
6-cyl, 2 ohc, or V12, ohc

CAPACITY
258 CID/4235cc;
326 CID/5343cc

MAXIMUM POWER
193/289bhp

CHASSIS/SUSPENSION
Separate tubular steel chassis frame; coil spring and wishbone ifs; coil spring, wishbone and fixed-length drive shaft irs

BODY STYLE
5 seater Cabriolet, by Panther

TOP SPEED
130mph/209kph approx

0-60MPH
8.5 seconds approx

During the 1970s, it became fashionable for small firms either to make accurate replicas of obsolete cars, or pastiches of a particular type. Panther Westwinds, in the UK, decided to produce pastiches, most of which were Jaguar-powered.

The first of this type was a two-seater sports car (the J72) which had something of the flavour, but none of the authenticity, of the SS100 of the 1930s, while the second was an altogether larger machine.

This car, the De Ville, used the same basic Jaguar mechanical equipment as had the J72 before it, but this time it had a Bugatti-like front grille, and was said to resemble a slightly modernized Bugatti Type 41 Royale. It was nothing like any of the six Royales (all of which have survived), and was flashily flamboyant rather than dignified, but it had a certain flair which appealed to a wealthy, if limited, clientele. A typical buyer was a pop star who wished to make an immediate impression, or a rich Middle Eastern client who had become bored with Rolls-Royce, Cadillac or Mercedes-Benz offerings.

The De Ville was built on a massive but simple tubular chassis frame, with a 142in/360.5cm wheelbase and with up-to-date Jaguar XJ12-type front and rear suspension, and in its original form it was sold only as a two-door saloon. As the body shell was constructed by traditional methods – there was a wooden skeleton, to which steel and light-alloy panels (mostly wheeled, or hand-beaten) were attached – it was quite straightforward for it to become a Cabriolet, and a few of these monstrously expensive machines were also built.

There was a choice of engines, both Jaguar – either the venerable six-cylinder XK unit in 4.2-litre/258 CID form or the more modern 5.3-litre/326 CID V12 – and in either case the car had impressive performance and equally daunting fuel consumption.

Because the Bugatti-style radiator grille was lofty and wide, and because the headlamps and the front wings all stood out on each side of the grille, the car looked even larger than it was. Viewed from the side, it had a horizontal waistline which finally dropped behind the rear wheel arches, where the exposed spare wheel was mounted.

A two-tone colour scheme was invariably specified, to break up the mass of the flanks. The screen was fixed, and there were wind-up windows in the doors. Even the headlamps gave a false impression, for inside their vast envelope there were more modern, and smaller, sealed-beam units.

If the De Ville had not been conceived at the height of the first Energy Crisis, and if Panther itself had not struck financial problems unrelated to this car, the De Ville might have sold better than it did. No development or styling changes were carried out during the 1970s, and the car died a natural death at about the time that the Panther company changed hands.

ABOVE Under the skin of the 1930s-style pastiche is modern Jaguar running gear. The Panther DeVille, some say, was inspired by the styling of large Bugattis.

TOP RIGHT The DeVille's front end is strongly reminiscent of a 1930s Supercar, but the chassis 'dumbiron covers' hide independent front suspension. The grille looks vaguely like that of a Bugatti, but there is no attempt to duplicate that car's mechanical equipment.

LEFT Look very carefully and you will see that the massive headlamps of the Panther DeVille actually enclose conventional modern lamps.

BELOW Most DeVilles were sold as two-door four-seater saloons, but a few, very exclusively, were bodied as Cabriolets.

PORSCHE 356 CABRIOLET

PRODUCTION SPAN
1949–1965

ENGINE
Flat-4, ohv

CAPACITY
66 CID/1086cc to 97 CID/1582cc

MAXIMUM POWER
40 to 90bhp

CHASSIS/SUSPENSION
Pressed platform chassis structure, with steel body shell, torsion bar and trailing link ifs, torsion bar and swing axle irs

BODY STYLE
2+2 seater Cabriolet, by Beutler/Porsche

TOP SPEED
85mph/137kph to 111mph/197kph, depending on engine

0-60MPH
15 seconds to 11.5 seconds, depending on engine

The name of Porsche had been famous for many years before the first Porsche car was launched. Dr Ferdinand Porsche had designed many fine cars for companies including Austro-Daimler and Mercedes-Benz before setting up his own design bureau in 1930. His crowning achievement in the 1930s, however, was to design the legendary VW 'Beetle', and it was on the basis of this car that his son Ferry developed the first Porsche-badged sports car, always known as the 356 model.

The first hand-built Porsches were produced in Austria, but proper series production began in 1949 when the company re-established itself in Stuttgart, West Germany. Almost from the start, the new rear-engined Porsches were available as Coupes or as Cabriolets.

In the beginning, these cars were little more than special-bodied VW Beetles, but as development progressed the engineering became more and more special. The flat-four air-cooled engines, in particular, soon became almost pure Porsche, and were much more powerful than any engine used in a VW-badged car.

The platform chassis had its engine in the tail, driving forward to a gearbox/transaxle, while there was independent suspension at front and rear. Most of the car's weight was in the rear, which led to early Porsches having a reputation for somewhat precarious handling, with lots of tail-out oversteer.

Following up the themes of the wind-cheating Beetle and the still-born sports coupe types which had been developed for VW in the late 1930s, Porsche produced a very smooth and slippery body style. The nose was very low, the headlamps were completely faired into the front wings and there was a continuous sweep of sheet metal from nose to tail.

Most early cars were fixed head/fastback coupes, but the Cabriolet, whose top tucked neatly away when furled, but which had a very small rear window, was also popular. Because this car had a relatively high waistline and low seating, one definitely sat 'in' rather than 'on' a Porsche 356.

There were four distinctly different types of 356 – the original vee-screen cars built up until 1955, the Type 356A of 1955-1959 (which had a one-piece screen), the 356Bs of 1959-1963, with raised headlamps and bumpers and the final Type 356C of 1963-1965, which had disc brakes. In that time the engines were gradually but persistently enlarged, with many different sizes being offered along the way. The majority of surviving 356s, however, now seem to have the 1582cc/96.6 CID engine, either in 75bhp or 90bhp guise.

All these Porsches had remarkably efficient body styles (the coupe being rather more wind-cheating than the Cabriolet) and because they were also high-geared it was possible to cruise along very quickly for hours on end. A Porsche of this type, too, was not only a fast car, but a very reliable car, and most customers, having bought their first, stayed loyal to Stuttgart for many car changes to come.

OPPOSITE Over the years the Porsche 356 was produced with several different body types. The Cabriolet was on sale from the start, and was later joined by a hardtop version using the same body pressings. The engine was in the tail, and much of the chassis engineering derived from that of the VW Beetle.

RIGHT, INSET Every detail of the Porsche's styling was carefully worked out, for there was a Porsche badge on the chrome handle, which was also used to lift up the lid of the front compartment.

OVERLEAF A historic Porsche – actually the first car produced by the fledgling firm in 1948. This was a very starkly detailed machine, which was almost entirely VW Beetle under the smooth skin.

PORSCHE

911 TARGA & CABRIOLET

PRODUCTION SPAN
1965 to date

ENGINE
Flat-6, ohc

CAPACITY
121 CID/1991cc to 201 CID/3299cc

MAXIMUM POWER
130 to 300bhp

CHASSIS/SUSPENSION
Unit-construction steel body/chassis structure, torsion bar and MacPherson strut ifs, torsion bar and semi-trailing arm irs

BODY STYLE
2+2 seater open-top 'Targa', or Cabriolet, by Porsche

TOP SPEED
137mph/220kph to 162mph/261kph, depending on engine

0-60MPH
8.0 seconds to 5.0 seconds, depending on engine

The Porsche 911 is probably the most successful Supercar of all time, not only for the performance which all derivatives offered, but for the reliability and service expertise built up around this long-running family of cars.

The 911 was conceived to supplement, then take over from, the long-running 356 family. It was announced in 1963 in 2.0-litre/121 CID form, and went on sale in 1964. Its design philosophy was exactly the same – rear-mounted air-cooled engine, wind-cheating style, 2+2 seating – but every single component was newly developed.

The original 911s were all 2+2-seater fastback coupes, but from the autumn of 1965 a new type of style, called 'Targa' was introduced. This, while keeping the same body lines, included a removable soft-top panel, while there was a substantial and permanently fixed roll-hoop above the occupants' heads. Even so, this was not a complete, conventional Cabriolet, and it was not until 1982 that such a fully convertible 911 was put on sale.

In its styling, the first 911 was a natural descendant of the final 356, with a low snout with headlamps at the corners, a fastback body style and a multitude of air vents in the tail. The whole car was rather wider, squatter, larger and subtly more upmarket than the earlier 356.

Over the years the style changed considerably, in detail if not in concept, for the wheelbase was slightly lengthened (which caused changes around the rear wheel arches), wheels and tyres were progressively widened (which resulted in the appearance of wheel-arch flares, front and rear), while aerodynamic 'tuning' resulted in the addition of substantial front under-bumper spoilers and a selection of large spoilers across the tail. In the same period the engine was gradually enlarged, eventually to 3.3-litres/201 CID, with a turbocharged version being sold from 1975.

The structure itself was a sturdy steel monocoque which, from the late 1970s, was largely made from galvanized panels. The engine was tucked away in the rear, and there was all-independent suspension, allied to four-wheel disc brakes and rack-and-pinion steering, to give the best possible roadholding from a layout with unpromising weight distribution. Early cars had spooky handling, but later cars, with wider wheels and tyres, were improved; the turbocharged cars were the fastest, and the best, of all.

Even though it was developed with Teutonic thoroughness, the 911 always retained a great deal of rather self-willed character. The combination of styling, performance, efficiency and above all the flat-sounding bark of the six-cylinder engine was unmatched by any rival. Time and again the 911 was rumoured to be on the verge of extinction (and indeed the front-engined 928 was originally designed to replace it), but it continued to sell as well as ever.

If Porsche was starting again, it would probably make the 911 a more spacious car with a quieter engine, but that might have resulted in a soulless car without hundreds of thousands of fanatical owners.

RIGHT Porsche put the 911 Coupe on sale in 1964, but the first open-top 'Targa' variety followed in 1965. The basic shape was not then changed for the next two decades as this study of a 1988 model confirms. The roll bar behind the seats is fixed, for only the roof panel can be removed.

FAR RIGHT A fully convertible of the famous Porsche 911 design was put on sale in 1982.

BELOW RIGHT More than 20 years after it was put on sale, the Porsche 911 still looked elegant and gracious. The engine was in the extreme tail, and even on full convertible types there was a comprehensively trimmed and equipped interior.

S JN 7386

S ET 2516

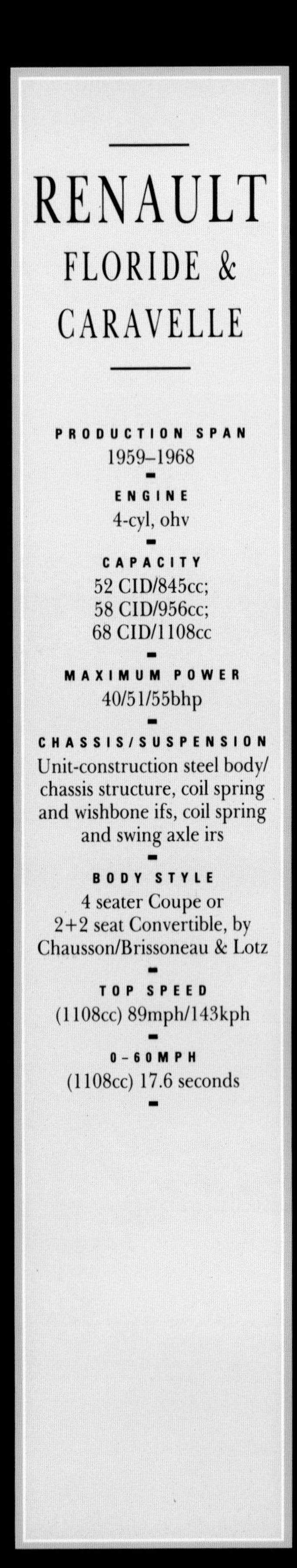

RENAULT
FLORIDE & CARAVELLE

PRODUCTION SPAN
1959–1968

ENGINE
4-cyl, ohv

CAPACITY
52 CID/845cc;
58 CID/956cc;
68 CID/1108cc

MAXIMUM POWER
40/51/55bhp

CHASSIS/SUSPENSION
Unit-construction steel body/chassis structure, coil spring and wishbone ifs, coil spring and swing axle irs

BODY STYLE
4 seater Coupe or 2+2 seat Convertible, by Chausson/Brissoneau & Lotz

TOP SPEED
(1108cc) 89mph/143kph

0-60MPH
(1108cc) 17.6 seconds

After the Second World War, Renault was nationalized by the French government, and for many years it concentrated on building conventional saloon cars. The vast majority of these were small, rear-engined machines, and it was from the second generation of this type that two sporty new cars, the Floride and Caravelle, were developed.

The 'donor' saloon, from which the sportier types were developed, was the curvacious Dauphine Gordini model, itself a sports saloon which had its four-cylinder water-cooled engine in the extreme tail, a very tail-heavy weight distribution and a reputation for rather skittish handling.

The original Floride of 1959 (called Caravelle in the USA market) used all the same running gear, and was built on the same underpan as the Dauphine Gordini but had attractive and more angular styling. The steel-panelled Floride was offered in hardtop coupe or convertible types, produced for Renault by Chausson, but with final body trim and final assembly by Brissoneau & Lotz. There was also a detachable hardtop option, which made the convertible look exactly like the coupe . . . .

At first this car used the 845cc/51.5 CID engine, but in 1962 the design was rejigged. There was a brand-new Renault family car – the R8 – in the offing, so the coupe/convertible twins were updated to include this car's new and larger engine, along with its four-wheel disc brakes, while the roof style of the fixed-head model was made more angular; soon afterwards the model name became Caravelle all over the world. By the end of 1963 that new engine had already been enlarged, to 1108cc/68 CID, and the development process was complete.

Because the Floride/Caravelle was a model with more glitz than performance, and with rather bright and glossy trim, it tended to be written off by the purists, and was even given that dreadful nickname of a 'hairdresser's car', yet it sold well, especially in France and other Mediterranean countries, and was a much more practical machine than many more expensive rivals. Even the final Caravelle was a brisk, rather than a fast, car, but it hummed along willingly unless grotesquely overloaded.

Compared with previous Renaults, the Floride/Caravelle was more obviously 'styled' rather than merely shaped, and featured headlamps located coyly in recesses (a detail said to have influenced MG's choice of the same feature for the MGB), sculptured flanks and a spacious 'engine deck' with air vents to allow hot air to get away from the engine bay itself. The coupe's rear seat was significantly larger than that of the convertible, because of the need to allow space for the soft top to be stowed away. There was also ample luggage space in the nose.

French fashions changed during the 1960s, with sporty salons taking more and more of the market, so when the Caravelle was dropped in 1968 it was not replaced. The next sporty Renault of this type was the R15/R17 range of coupes in the early 1970s.

RIGHT Tucked away in the tail, with only louvres in the lift-up panel to give the game away, the Caravelle had an overhead valve four-cylinder engine, and four speed transmission.

BELOW RIGHT Stylists, no doubt, would dismissively date this facia as 1960s; but what further information does any driver need?

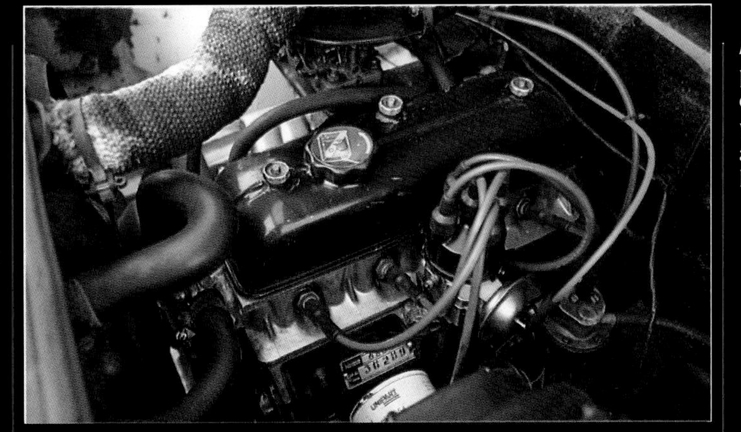

BELOW Although it isn't easy to produce a graceful style on a rear-engined car, Renault succeeded with the Caravelle. A bigger engine and more performance would have made it a more desirable car.

ROLLS-ROYCE PHANTOM II & 20/25

PRODUCTION SPAN
1929–1936

ENGINE
6-cyl, ohv

CAPACITY
225 CID/3699cc;
468 CID/7668cc

MAXIMUM POWER
Never quoted

CHASSIS/SUSPENSION
Ladder-type separate steel chassis, half-elliptic leaf spring and beam front, half-elliptic spring and beam rear

BODY STYLE
2 to 7 seater Drop-head Coupes, Tourers or Landaulettes, by specialist coachbuilders

TOP SPEED
(20/25) 70mph/113kph;
(Phantom II) 90mph/145kph

0-60MPH
(20/25) 35 seconds;
(Phantom II) 20-24 seconds

Introduced at a time when the world's economies were turning down and when the rich were suddenly not so well off as before, the costly and luxurious Rolls-Royce 20/25 and Phantom II models had a difficult task ahead of them. By that time, however, it was enough that they *were* Rolls-Royce cars, and their purchase was usually considered to be an investment rather than an indulgence.

A pedant would no doubt insist that there was no such thing as a complete Rolls-Royce at that time, as the company only built complete rolling chassis for completion by specialist coachbuilders. The fact is, however, that the Derby-based company usually (but not always) managed to steer its customers discreetly towards favoured coachbuilders such as H. J. Mulliner, Park Ward, Hooper, Barker and a handful of body makers in Europe.

The Rolls-Royce chassis of the day, whether 'large' (Phantom II) or 'small' (20/25hp) was conventional, but exquisitely built. Engines were low-revving six-cylinder units, brake operation was assisted by the Hispano-type of mechanical servo, while front and rear suspension was by half-elliptic springs and lever-arm dampers.

Rolls-Royce completed the chassis, which then could be (and often was) driven to the chosen coachbuilder. With the chassis came the company's famous Palladian-style radiator, as well as the scuttle-firewall and instrument panel, both retained at the company's insistence.

Every type of body was, of course, married to these chassis, ranging from staid and upright limousines with divisions, through rakish 'owner-driver' sports saloons, to any number of startlingly elegant open-top machines. Cars that seemed to be limousines were often Landaulettes, coupes were sometimes instantly transformable into dropheads, while many customers insisted on tourers, some looking rather upright, some looking very sporty indeed.

Although a few startlingly inappropriate body styles slipped through, most of these shells were tasteful, nicely detailed and carefully assembled. Invariably the shell was built up around a skeleton of seasoned hard wood, and on many occasions the hand-beaten panelling would be in rust-proof light alloy. Wings and running boards, however, were usually in steel, which was better able to withstand the assault of stones from the road surface.

The variety, and the sheer inventiveness of the coachbuilders concerned, was a joy. Some cars had one or even two exposed spare wheels tucked into recesses in front wings, some had integral luggage boots but others used demountable containers, some used wheel discs, others left their wire-spoke wheels exposed. All had massive headlamps at each side of the grille, that famous radiator and the 'Spirit of Ecstasy' on the prow.

At the time, Rolls-Royce motoring was a dignified, rather than a hurried, process, so these cars (especially the 20/25s) were by no means as fast and powerful as they looked. The queue to buy them, however, never disappeared.

RIGHT Look carefully at this exquisitely bodied Phantom II, and it becomes obvious why every gentleman wanted to be seen in one in the 1930s. All the details are typical of a twenties/thirties coachbuilt style, including the mounting of the spare wheel on the side of the body.

BELOW RIGHT Coachbuilders produced a huge variety of styles for the 20/25 chassis, not only open-top but saloons and limousines. All of them were graceful and dignified.

GC 2153

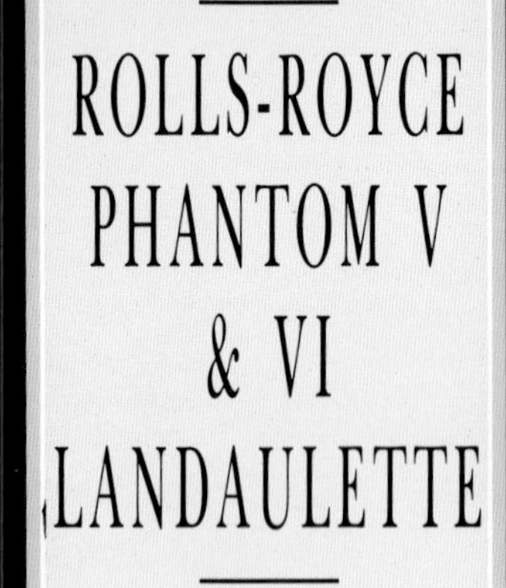

ROLLS-ROYCE PHANTOM V & VI LANDAULETTE

PRODUCTION SPAN
1962 to date

ENGINE
V8, ohv

CAPACITY
380 CID/6230cc or
412 CID/6750cc

MAXIMUM POWER
Never quoted

CHASSIS/SUSPENSION
Ladder chassis frame, with cruciform members, coil spring and wishbone ifs, half-elliptic leaf spring rear

BODY STYLE
7 seater Landaulette, by Mulliner Park Ward

TOP SPEED
100mph/161kph to 105mph/169kph, depending on engine

0-60MPH
14 seconds

The Rolls-Royce tradition of building magnificently bodied Phantoms has never faltered. The first of the post-war limousines, in fact, were Silver Wraiths, but these were soon joined by a very exclusive series of straight-eight Phantom IVs. In 1959 the long-running Silver Wraith was retired, and immediately replaced by the massive yet elegant Phantom V. Each and every Phantom V, and the Phantom VIs which took over in 1968, was coachbuilt.

The Phantom V had the larger and longer-wheelbase, derivative of the S-Series chassis which made its debut in 1955, and was upgraded to SZ-specification with the brand-new light-alloy V8 engine in 1959. Standard steel saloons had a wheelbase of 123in/312cm, whereas the Phantom's wheelbase was stretched considerably, to 145in/368cm.

At first, the Phantom V was offered with a choice of several body styles, most being by Mulliner Park Ward, Hooper, or James Young. Some were limousines with divisions (to be driven by chauffeurs) and some were 'touring limousines', which meant that they had no division and were often driven by their owners. Every car was large, spacious, dignified and signalled its approach by that patrician and quite unmistakable radiator style.

The Phantom was too large a car for a full convertible body style to be thought practical or elegant. Rolls-Royce therefore evolved a half-and-half design in which most of the shell remained closed but the rear section could be opened up. This long-established style was, and is, known as a Landaulette.

The first Landaulette derivative of the Phantom V was built by Mulliner Park Ward in 1962, and delivered to H.M. The Queen Mother. For this car, there was a fold-down soft top above and behind the rear seats only. Later, Rolls-Royce offered a slightly different version, in which the folding roof was longer, and was fixed to the top of the division between front and rear compartments. This car also had an electrically operated rear seat which could, if needed, be raised by 3.5in/8.9cm. They were, need it be said, extremely exclusive machines.

All the statistics were large, and impressive, for a typical Phantom V Landaulette was 19ft 10in/624cm long, weighed about 5,600lb/2,540kg and rarely seemed to record better than 10 Imperial mpg. As to price – well, gentlemen never discuss money, do they? Like all such 'ceremonial' Rolls-Royces, they were cars in which to be seen, and in which to be driven around town, or from public engagement and board meeting to the town house or country dwelling, rather than as regular, long-distance, business transport.

The Phantom V became the Phantom VI in 1968, with minor changes. The enlarged 6.75-litre/412 CID engine soon followed, and in 1978 the chassis was given the high-tech hydraulic circuitry of the Silver Shadow. Even so, the styling of the Mulliner Park Ward limousines and Landaulettes never changed, and a late 1980s car looked almost identical to a 1960s example.

RIGHT The coachwork of this Phantom VI was by Mulliner Park Ward, Rolls Royce's own body building subsidiary. Most cars were limousines, but an exclusive handful were given open (rear) landaulette styling.

FAR RIGHT Almost by tradition, the division of a coachbuilt Rolls-Royce featured a great deal of immaculately polished wood, and a cocktail cabinet. Rolls-Royce provided the crystal, but customers were expected to provide their own drinks.

BELOW RIGHT Although it had graceful and dignified lines, the Phantom VI was a *very* large car, nearly 20 feet long. There was ample room for five in the rear compartment, though only those sitting in the rear seat itself got the benefit of the open-top when it was furled.

12
10
12
JHX 178N

SAAB 900

CABRIOLET TURBO 16

PRODUCTION SPAN
1986 to date

ENGINE
4-cyl, 2 ohc

CAPACITY
121 CID/1985cc

MAXIMUM POWER
175bhp

CHASSIS/SUSPENSION
Steel unit-construction body shell, coil spring and wishbone ifs, coil spring and radius arm rear.

BODY STYLE
4 seater Cabriolet, by Saab-Finland

TOP SPEED
125mph/201kph

0-60MPH
8.5 seconds

Having started out as a car maker, with two-stroke engines and front-wheel drive, Saab progressed rapidly. A new generation of passenger cars, the Saab 99, was introduced in 1967, and this was greatly refined, as the longer-wheelbase Saab 900, in 1978. Saab's first 'own-design' engine was launched in 1972, and was a 2-litre/121 CID overhead-cam 'four'. The same basic engine, in a much refined and more developed form, was still the mainstay of Saab's line-up in the late 1980s.

Saab had been selling cars for more than 30 years before it considered building a convertible, this being inspired by requests from Saab-USA for a new model to satisfy the continuing demand for open-top cars in North America.

By the time the prototype Cabriolet was shown in 1983, the 900 family had already been on sale for five years. Since the car was being sold in hatchback and salon styles, with a whole variety of engine tunes including a powerful turbocharged version, it was reasonable that a Saab spokesman should quip: 'There wasn't much left we could do but take the roof off!'

Although Saab's design centre produced the car, much expertise for the conversion came from the American Sunroof Company. After the car had been shown in 1983, it took well over two years before it could go on sale, with manufacture taking place at the Saab-Finland factory at Uusikaupunki.

Because Saab saw the Cabriolet as its most prestigious model, it was not only given full air-conditioning for sale in the USA, and a power-operated soft top, but also it had an ingeniously arranged glass rear window which dropped into a pouch ahead of the boot when the soft top was being furled.

The engine chosen was the very latest twin-overhead-camshaft turbocharged 2-litre/121 CID unit, which had four valves per cylinder and pushed out no less than 175bhp (or 160bhp in USA-sale form). This gave the Cabriolet a sparkling performance which would attract any traffic policeman for miles.

Compared with the Saab saloons, the Cabriolet had slightly reduced four-seater accommodation, but its underside was reinforced to leave the body as stiff as before. Unlike some Cabriolets, the soft top furled neatly, and almost completely, to waist level, and there was complete all-round visibility behind a large (saloon-sized) front screen when this had been done.

Like its saloon and hatchback counterparts, the 900 Cabriolet had sporty front-wheel-drive roadholding, that minor but unmistakable turbo 'whine' under the bonnet and every possible safety fitting for which Swedish car makers are noted.

BOTTOM Except that there was the inevitable visibility blind spot in the rear quarters, the 900 Cabriolet Turbo 16 was a thoroughly practical convertible car: customers seemed to think it was well worth the premium price asked.

TOP Saab's 900 Cabriolet used the same basic body structure as the saloons, but the conversion was engineered by the American Sunroof Company.

MIDDLE The badging – 900 Turbo – reminded the world not only that this was a soft-top car, but that it also had the performance of a turbocharged sports saloon.

RIGHT American Sunroof went to a great deal of trouble to make the Saab 900 a refined soft-top model. With the soft-top erect it was as snug and weather-proof as the saloons, and to emphasise this point it was sold with full air-conditioning as standard.

TOYOTA MR2 T-BAR

PRODUCTION SPAN
1986 to date

ENGINE
4-cyl, ohc or 2 ohc

CAPACITY
89 CID/1453cc or
97 CID/1587cc

MAXIMUM POWER
83, 130 or 145bhp

CHASSIS/SUSPENSION
Steel unit-construction body shell, coil spring and MacPherson strut ifs, coil spring and MacPherson strut irs

BODY STYLE
2 seater removable-roof model,by Toyota

TOP SPEED
108mph/173kph;
124mph/200kph;
130mph/209kph,
depending on engine

0-60MPH
(130bhp model) 7.7 seconds

Although Toyota became one of Japan's largest car makers in the 1960s and 1970s, it made little attempt to produce ultra-sporting machinery; instead its effort was concentrated on producing millions of family cars. Then, in the early 1980s, the emphasis changed – not only were new families of multi-valve twin-cam engines produced, but the new models became progressively more interesting.

One of the most advanced sports cars of the 1970s had been the mid-engined Fiat X1/9, so when Toyota decided to produce its own small sports car it was no surprise to see that the same basic layout was chosen. (At the same time, by the way, Pontiac engineers also completed the same sort of job, the result being the mid-engined Fiero model.) The new Toyota, called MR2 (for Midship Runabout), was launched in 1984, and an open-top version, the T-Roof type, was put on sale in 1986.

Like the Fiat X1/9 before it, the MR2 was something of a miracle of packaging, for although the four-cylinder engine and its transmission were mounted immediately behind the passenger cabin, there was luggage stowage space at the front *and* in the tail, as well as comfortable two-seater accommodation. In its original form the MR2 was a closed coupe (with a glass sun-roof, or 'moon-roof' option), but from 1986 a T-Roof model was added to the range.

As with other T-Bar models, such as the Nissan/Datsun Z-Car type, the car's styling was virtually unchanged, but there was a permanently fixed bar between the front screen rail and the bodywork above and behind the seats; this was done to retain the original car's body rigidity. On each side of this T-Bar, and placed directly above the seats, were removable glass roof panels; when these were out, and with the side windows wound down, the MR2 was almost, but not quite, converted into an open-top car. In general, the MR2 had a wedge-nose front, with pop-up headlamps, a stubby tail and a large transverse spoiler at the rear to help trim the handling.

Toyota offered a choice of engines, the most powerful of which was a supercharged (*not* turbocharged) 1.6-litre/97 CID unit pushing out 145bhp, and all types had true sports-car handling characteristics and character. As you might expect from a modern Japanese car, the MR2 was carefully built, well backed by service and spares, and brought back the joys of open-top motoring to those who didn't want to have to cosset their cars.

INSET, RIGHT The MR2 was a neatly conceived two-seater package, in effect an update of Fiat's X1/9.

INSET, MIDDLE This view of the MR2 suggests the power behind the bustle; perhaps they aren't Ferrari-smooth, but there's an impressive sense of purpose in those lines.

INSET, FAR RIGHT Two comfortable seats, and not much room for anything else but two bodies. The MR2 is designed for a purpose, and that means carrying only two people.

RIGHT Are you old enough to remember when, back in the 1960s, Japanese stylists' efforts were often criticised by the European and American pundits? It doesn't happen any more, and with good reason, as this study of the MR2's front end, with its neatly lidded headlamps, shows.

D282 HYN
TOYOTA
D282 HYN

TOYOTA

LEFT The MR2's well-designed instrument display with 'everything to hand', as the brochures usually say.

MIDDLE Detail of the MR2's matching speedometer and rev-counter dials.

BOTTOM The MR2's nose is empty, except for the spare wheel and offers space to stow the removable roof panels if the mood takes you in mid-journey.

INSET, LEFT The MR2 with its roof panels removed is open-top, but still has all the rigidity of a coupe.

LEFT AND LEFT BELOW These views offer little evidence of the MR2's T-Bar feature. The engine is transversely mounted behind the cockpit.

TRIUMPH

TR4, TR4A, TR5, TR250

PRODUCTION SPAN
1961–1968

ENGINE
4-cyl, ohv, or 6-cyl, ohv

CAPACITY
121 CID/1991cc;
130 CID/2138cc;
152 CID/2498cc

MAXIMUM POWER
83, 130 or 145bhp

CHASSIS/SUSPENSION
Separate frame, coil spring and wishbone ifs, half-elliptic rear on TR4, coil spring and semi-trailing irs on others

BODY STYLE
2 seater Roadster, or removable-roof model, by Standard-Triumph

TOP SPEED
102mph/164kph;
109mph/175kph;
120mph/193kph,
depending on engine

0-60MPH
10.9 seconds to 8.8 seconds, depending on model

The first Triumph TR to go on sale was the TR2 of 1953, and the same 'side-curtain' body style then remained in production for nine years. It was with this light, rugged and characterful little car that Triumph made its reputation in the USA.

Whereas the TR2/TR3/TR3A range had been strictly conventional, even traditional, in its body layout, the car which succeeded it in 1961 was much more adventurous. Not only was the TR4 a better-equipped and more civilized machine than any previous TR, but it had particularly versatile features. The secret of the new car, which had been conceived and styled by Giovanni Michelotti in Italy, was not only that it had wind-up windows in the doors, along with face-level ventilation on the instrument panel, but also that it was the first car to use the removable-roof type of hardtop which was later credited to Porsche.

The same basic body shell was used in four TR models in the 1960s, but there were important mechanical differences between them all. The TR4 used a slightly modified version of the TR3A's 88in/223.5cm wheelbase chassis, still using the famous 'wet-liner' four-cylinder engine which was also used in the Standard Vanguard family car, and the Ferguson tractor! This chassis still had limited wheel movement and a very hard ride. In 1965, the TR4A had a new chassis, with independent rear suspension (except in the USA where an old-style beam axle was optional). Then in 1967, the TR5 and TR250 models were given smooth new 2498cc/152.5 CID six-cylinder engines (developed from the Triumph 2000), with fuel injection for the TR5 and a de-toxed engine for the TR250.

The most exciting and extroverted of all these types was the TR5, which had a genuine top speed of around 120mph/193kph, acceleration to match, and character which really required a strong-armed and strong-willed driver to get the best out of it.

In its normal 'Roadster' form, the TR4 and its successors had a normal fold-down soft top, which was covered in a bag when furled. The cars were also sold with optional hardtops, and it was here that innovation appeared. The removable hardtop was a two-piece, bolt-together item, comprising a rear section surrounding the rear window, and a complete steel roof panel which could be removed and left at home, if desired. Not only that, but a 'Surrey top' could also be supplied, which was a soft top on a light tubular frame which could be fitted in place of the steel roof panel. In full hard-top form, with steel roof in place and with windows wound up, these cars were as wind- and waterproof as a saloon, but with everything off they were still proper sports cars.

For 1969 this body shell was considerably facelifted by Karmann of West Germany to become the TR6, but there was a new and angular hardtop option, without removable panels and without the ability to chop and change according to the driver's wishes.

RIGHT The Michelotti-styled TR4 was introduced in 1961, and also provided the body style for later versions, the TR4A and the TR5/TR250 models. This is a TR5, dating from 1967, and has the optional hardtop fitted, but with the centre panel removed.

FAR RIGHT Triumph provided the original 'Targa' type of open-top motoring before Porsche re-invented it for its 911 models. The rear half of the optional hardtop is fixed to the body shell, and the roof can be a steel panel, or a canvas 'Surrey' top.

BELOW RIGHT Under the skin of all such TRs was a separate steel chassis frame. For the TR4A, the independent rear suspension was new, while the TR5 and TR250 models were the first to use six-cylinder engines.

OFN 808F
OFN 808F

TRIUMPH STAG

PRODUCTION SPAN
1970–1977

ENGINE
V8, ohv

CAPACITY
183 CID/2997cc

MAXIMUM POWER
145bhp

CHASSIS/SUSPENSION
Unit-construction monocoque shell, coil spring and MacPherson strut ifs, coil spring and semi-trailing arm irs

BODY STYLE
4 seater Convertible, or with removable hardtop, by Standard-Triumph

TOP SPEED
116mph/187kph

0-60MPH
10.7 seconds

The Triumph Stag which appeared in 1970 was not the car which Michelotti had conceived in the mid-1960s, nor was it the car which Standard-Triumph had originally hoped to launch in 1968. By that time it had inherited a V8 engine, become more complex and more specialized, and was gunning for a new, up-market, sector which was quite unknown to Standard-Triumph.

In the beginning, the Stag started out as a one-off project car, a plaything cobbled up by Michelotti, in Turin, as a convertible version of the Triumph 2000 saloon. Even in that form, however, it was promising enough to be snapped up by Standard-Triumph for development as a production car.

The original prototype was a spacious five-seater built on the Triumph 2000's wheelbase, but for its production programme Triumph decided to shorten the wheelbase to 100in/254cm, turn it into a close-coupled four-seater, and use a fuel-injected TR5 type of engine. Then, as the Stag grew heavier and more highly specified, came another strategy change – the six-cylinder engine was discarded, in favour of the new 90-degree V8 Triumph unit. In production form, after much modification, it became a 145bhp 2997cc/183 CID unit which was not always completely reliable.

The Stag, in production form, had nose and tail styling rather like that of the 2000/2.5PI Mk 2 saloons, with four headlamps and a sharp tail cut-off, as well as a very similar wood-panelled instrument panel, steering wheel and controls. It had a beautifully trimmed and equipped interior, which included reclining front seats, two large passenger doors with front quarter lights, and wind-up windows.

In basic form, the Stag was sold as a convertible, with a fold-away soft top which, when furled, was stowed away under a hinged metal tonneau. A very popular option, however, was a sturdy steel hardtop which included glass rear quarter windows and a glass backlight.

In both cases, to add to the rigidity of the shell and to afford roll-over protection for the occupants, what became known as a 'T-bar' was tied to the centre of the windscreen rail and to the top of the pillars behind the door opening. This was trimmed and padded, and was an integral part of the design, being covered by the soft top (when erect) or the hardtop (when fitted). In spite of the inviting shape of the T-bar, Triumph never took the opportunity to add glass panels in the roof of the hardtop itself.

Compared with the related saloons, the Stag had more performance, and a unique V8 engine. It was a car which made no sacrifices in comfort in order to be an open-top machine, and when the running gear was in good condition, it was an excellent, high-geared Grand Tourer. Many of the cars were sold with automatic transmission, and many had smart cast-alloy road wheels.

When the saloons were withdrawn in 1977 the Stag died with them, and it was never replaced.

ABOVE The Stag was an appealing 2+2 seater package, with a V8 engine, all independent suspension, and a choice of soft-top or hard-top body styles.

LEFT All Triumph Stags were built with a stout 'T-bar' brace connecting the screen to a roll cage. The soft-top, when erect, fitted over the top of this.

LOWER LEFT The Stag had a beautifully equipped interior, with a wooden facia panel, and lavishly padded seating.

TVR
CONVERTIBLES

PRODUCTION SPAN
1981 to date

ENGINE
4-cyl ohc, V6 ohv, V8 ohv

CAPACITY
122 CID/1993cc;
170 CID/2792cc;
215 CID/3528cc
238 CID/3905cc

MAXIMUM POWER
101/160/190/275bhp

CHASSIS/SUSPENSION
Multi-tubular chassis frame, coil spring and wishbone ifs, coil spring and wishbone irs

BODY STYLE
2 seater Convertible, by TVR

TOP SPEED
Up to 144mph/232kph, depending on model

0-60MPH
Down to 5.6 seconds, depending on model

TVR is one of those small, specialist British car makers which seems to have had a charmed life. In 30 years of production at Blackpool, it has produced a whole variety of models, suffered serious financial crises, but is still around. The 1980s-generation of sports cars is not only fast and smart, but sells better and better with every year which passes.

When TVR started up, it build two-seater cars with multi-tube 'backbone' chassis frames, glass-fibre bodies and proprietary engines. Three decades on, and several design generations later, that approach has not changed.

The first of the modern generation of TVRs was announced in January 1980 as a hatchback coupe, but within two years the same 94in/239cm wheelbase chassis was also supporting a cramped 2+2-seater coupe, and a new two-seater Convertible. Since then, and with several different engines, the Convertible has become dominant at Blackpool, with almost all export orders being for that type of car. The original engine was a 2.8-litre/170 CID Ford-Germany V8. There were a few 2-litre/122 CID Ford 'fours', but the majority of all recent TVRs used the famous ex-Buick light-alloy Rover V8 unit; it was with that engine, in fuel-injected and often in tuned-up form, that the TVR Convertibles were most exciting of all.

As with all such TVRs, the Convertible's chassis frame was a multi-tube design, with four backbone tubes cradling the engine and transmission, and ensuring a sizable transmission tunnel inside the cockpit. There was independent front and rear suspension, rack-and-pinion steering, four-wheel disc brakes, a hard ride, generous helpings of the right noises and the right sort of 'seat-of-the-pants' feeling. The body shell was built up from glass-fibre panels, and unlike the TVR coupes the Convertible had a small, lockable luggage container in the tail. Its long and low snout, allied to a high bustle at the rear, was quite unmistakable.

When fully folded down, the soft top allowed the TVR to be a completely open car, but there was a solid safety roll hoop incorporated into the soft top which gave as much protection as a Porsche 'Targa' bar.

Names varied, for the 'Tasmin' title was gradually dropped in the mid-1980s in favour of plain titles like '280i' or '350i' which, with an extra '0' added in front of the 'i' (for fuel injection) denoted the car's engine size. Performance ranged from enterprising (130mph/209kph for the 280i) through to astonishing (144mph/232kph for the much-breathed-upon 3.9-litre/238 CID Rover-engined 390i), and every car had brakes, controllability and responses to match its straight-line performance. For the enthusiastic owner, the best possible feature was the glass-fibre body shell, which was rust-proof and easily repaired after minor scrapes.

RIGHT TVR built its first Convertible in 1978, and the same basic style, much modified and refined, was revived in 1986. This is the later 'S' type model, which got off to a flying start.

BELOW RIGHT The sharply detailed TVR 390SE was a further development of the Tasmin Convertible of 1981. Like all TVRs, this had a multi-tubular chassis frame, and glass-fibre body.

TVR
390 SE
390 SE
390 SE

VW
GOLF GTI CONVERTIBLE

PRODUCTION SPAN
1979 to date

ENGINE
4-cyl ohc

CAPACITY
97 CID/1588cc;
109 CID/1781cc

MAXIMUM POWER
110/112bhp

CHASSIS/SUSPENSION
Steel unit-construction body shell, coil spring and MacPherson strut ifs, coil spring and trailing arm irs

BODY STYLE
4 seater Cabriolet, by Karmann

TOP SPEED
113mph/182kph

0-60MPH
8.5 seconds

VW's business was founded on the building of millions of ugly, rear-engined, air-cooled saloons, the ubiquitous 'Beetles'. This car was only forced out of existence, in West Germany (but not in the rest of the world), by the arrival of the new Golf.

There was no possible comparison between Golf and Beetle – except that the Golf also became a best seller, by any world standards. After 40 years of design stagnation, VW jumped right up to date, launching a range of cars with transversely mounted engines at the front of the car driving the front wheels, and all having smart hatchback body styles by Giugiaro of Italy.

The Golf (and its elegant hatchback coupe, the Scirocco) went on sale in 1974, but there were no plans to make a convertible car at first. There was, however, a much faster and more powerful version, the 110bhp fuel-injected GTI, in the wings, this eventually going on sale in 1976.

A Cabriolet version of the monocoque Golf eventually surfaced in 1979, this new model having been styled, developed, tooled *and* put into production by the specialist coachbuilders, Karmann. Much of the standard car's body shell, and all the same running gear, were retained, but considerable stiffening was needed to keep the chopped-off shell strong enough to meet all safety requirements.

Because all the seating had to be retained, the Cabriolet lost almost all the boot space available in the hatch, but this was a minor penalty to pay for a very smart little four-seater. A small compartment, with a separate boot lid, was retained, and there was a box-section roll-over bar from pillar to pillar to add to the car's specification.

The Golf Cabriolet, if for no other reason, is important as the first of the modern generation of Convertibles, almost all of which are conversions, or re-engineering projects, based on mass-produced saloons or hatchbacks. For that reason one can forgive its tiny amount of stowage space, and the fact that the soft top folds back, but not out of sight, to give enjoyable open-air motoring.

The soft top itself was carefully developed so that it could be lowered in a matter of five seconds, and re-erected in little more. There were rigid cant-rails above the two passenger doors, and except for the lack of three-quarter rear visibility it almost approximated a two-door saloon when the soft top was erect.

As with the Golf hatchbacks, various engine sizes and power ratings were offered in the Golf Cabriolet, but the most desirable of all were those with the fuel-injected GTI engines. At first these were 1.6-litre/97 CID units, but a 1788cc/109 CID version was made available in the early 1980s. Even though the Golf hatchback itself was completely redesigned in 1983, the original and much-loved Cabriolet style of 1979 carried on into the late 1980s.

INSET VW Golf Cabriolets are specially-converted versions of the hatchback, still with four-seat accommodation, but losing out a little in terms of luggage space.

BELOW RIGHT In 1979 VW virtually re-invented the soft-top car for family motoring, this being an extensively redesigned version of the famous hatchback; it was built, for VW, by the coachbuilders Karmann.

GTI
D101 CBD

INDEX

Page numbers in *italics* refer to captions

F

G

H

I

J

K

L

M

N

O

P

PICTURE CREDITS

BMW p 7. Performance Car Magazine p 8. Midland Motor Museum p 9 (top). Chris Harvey p 9 (bottom). J Baker Collection pp 11, 12, 13, 15, 20, 21, 22, 23, 36, 37, 41, 47 (bottom), 53, 55, 56, 57, 59 (below), 67, 69, 71, 72, 75, 77, 81, 83 (top), 85 (top), 87 (top and middle), 91, 92, 93, 95, 97, 99, 106, 107, 113, 115, 116, 117, 119, 121, 125. Rolls Royce Motors pp 17, 19, 109. General Motors (Cadillac) pp 25, 27, 29. General Motors (Chevrolet) pp 31, 33. Chrysler Corporation p 35. Nissan Japan p 39. Harrah Auto Collection pp 43, 44. Ferrari pp 47 (top), 49, 51. Bertone Italy p 59 (above). Long Island Automotive Museum p 61. Ford Motor Company pp 63, 65, 79. Mercedes Benz pp 83 (bottom), 85 (bottom), 87 (bottom), 89. Porsche Cars pp 101, 102, 105. Frank Dale p 111. TVR p 123.